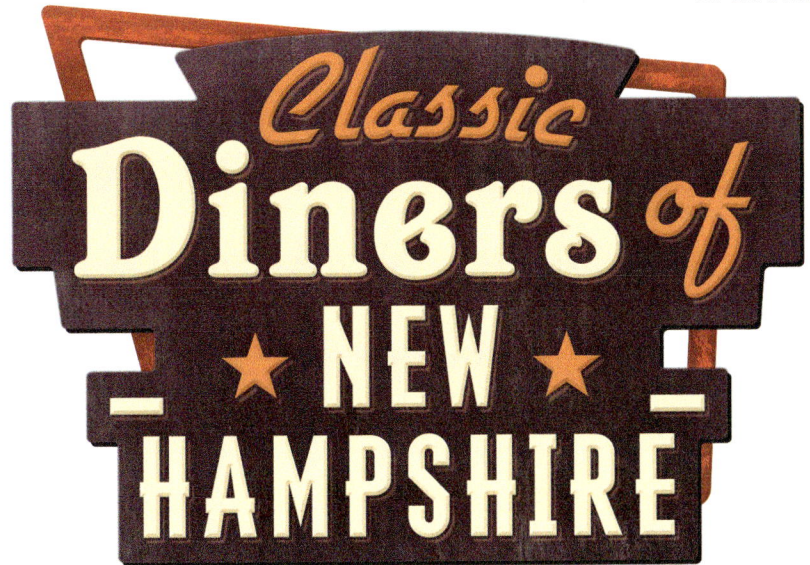

BRUCE D. HEALD, PhD

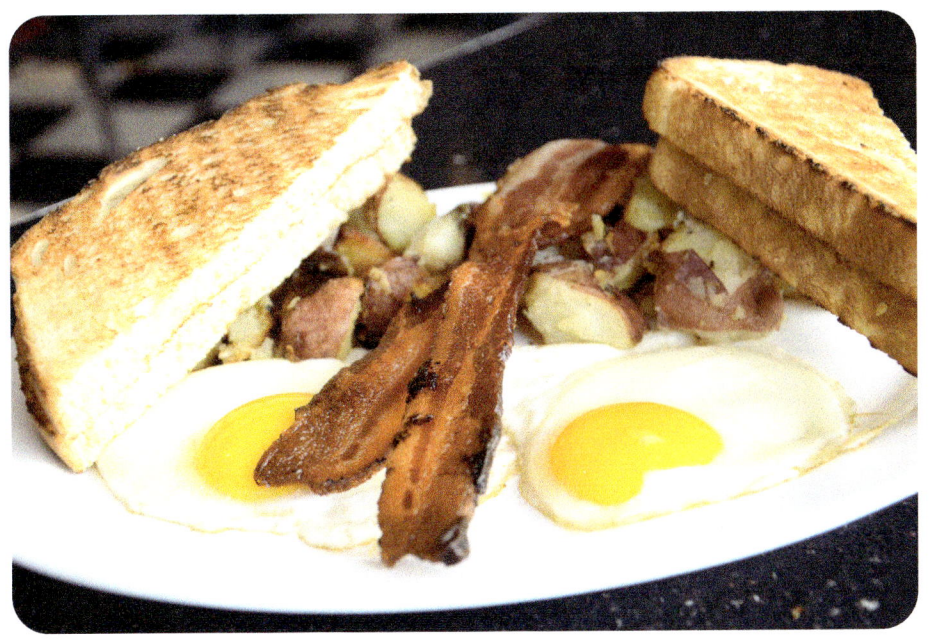

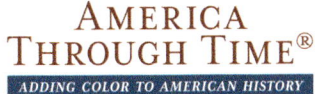

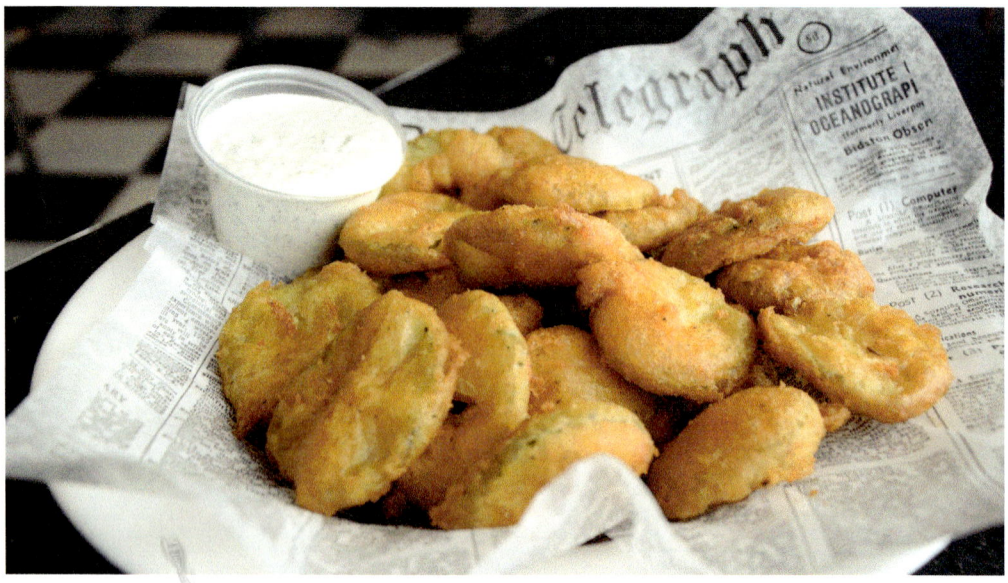

Fried pickles at the Roundabout, Portsmouth. On previous page, eggs and bacon at the Roundabout.

Credits

American Diner Museum, Jane Andrews, Scott Braham, Wayne Brink, Conway Scenic Railroad, Larry Cultreru, Teri Dunn, Mike Flynn, Bruce Fuller, Carol Lawrence, Joseph Manzo, Casondra Marden, Olde Bay Diner, Kimberly Ripley, Alex Ray and the Tilt'n Diner. The Roundabout Diner, Ron Scully, Marybeth Shanahan, Warren Watson, Barbara Westergaard.

America Through Time is an imprint of Fonthill Media LLC
www.through-time.com
books@through-time.com

Published by Arcadia Publishing by arrangement with Fonthill Media LLC
For all general information, please contact Arcadia Publishing:
Telephone: 843-853-2070
Fax: 843-853-0044

E-mail: sales@arcadiapublishing.com
For customer service and orders:
Toll-Free 1-888-313-2665

First published 2014. Reprinted 2021.

Copyright © Bruce Heald 2014, 2021

ISBN 978-1-62545-073-9

All rights reserved. No part of this publication may be reproduced, stored in a retrieval system or transmitted in any form or by any means, electronic, mechanical, photocopying, recording or otherwise, without prior permission in writing from Fonthill Media LLC.

Typeset in 10pt on 13pt Mrs Eaves
Printed and bound in England

Contents

	Introduction	5
1	The Origin of the New Hampshire Diners—1872 to 1930s	7
2	The Classic Diner Era—1940s to 1980s	9
3	Cultural Significance and Marketplace	11
4	Manufacturing the Classic Car Diners—Construction, Style and Design	14
5	List of Classic Diners in New Hampshire	21
6	List of Non-Classic Diners of New Hampshire	64
7	Railroad Diners	77
8	Reminiscences of the Diner	82
9	Trivia	90
	List of Diners in New Hampshire	93
	Bibliography	96

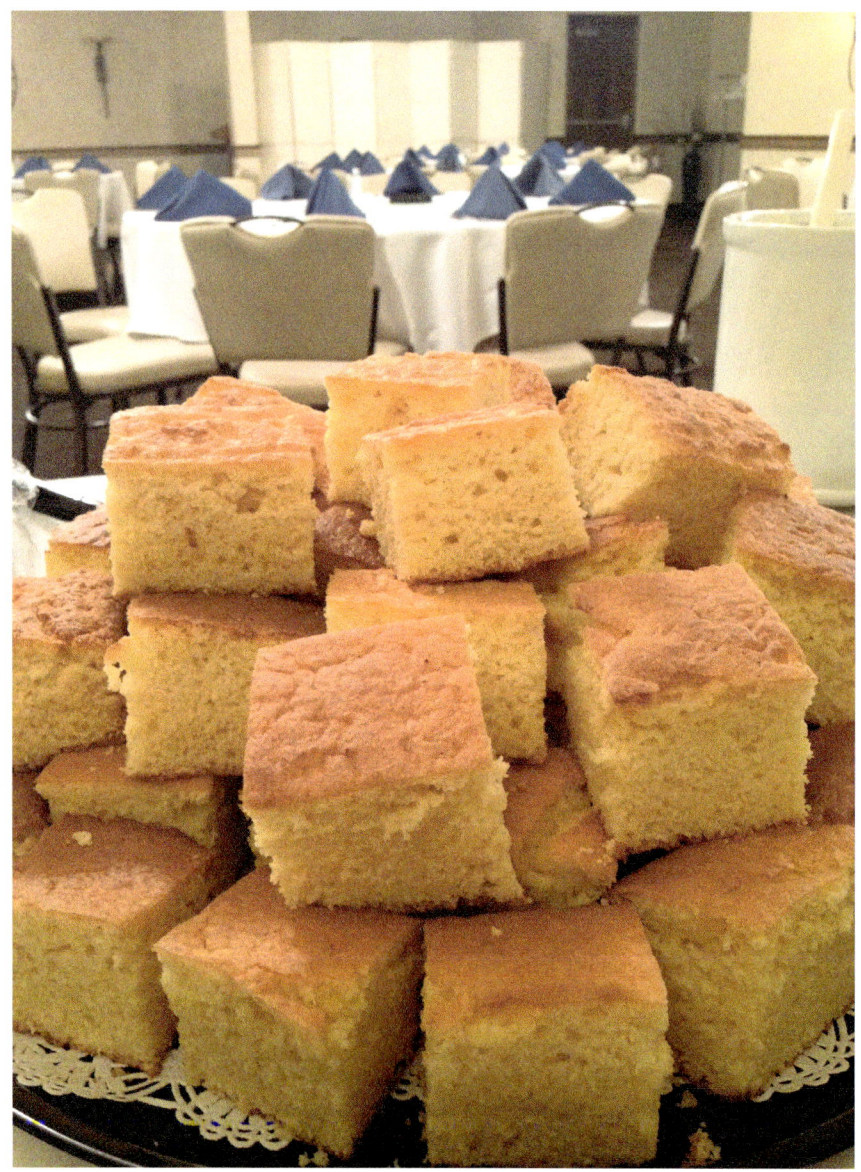
Cornbread at the Roundabout, Portsmouth.

Introduction

The diner exemplifies the uniqueness of the American spirit. It is the product of our culture and lifestyle. During the glory days of the lunch wagon—the late 1800s through the 1950s—it seemed that most every neighborhood had a diner. It was here in America that they were invented and evolved and flourished, from the wheeled lunch wagons, to the classic stainless-steel "streamliners." The diner defined who we were. Historian Richard Gutman wrote it perfectly in his book *American Diner*:

> They exemplify many of the best American qualities: free enterprise and entrepreneurship, mobility, our love of gadgets and machines—they were fitted out like a ship with everything in its place—the emphasis on convenience and, most of all, democracy. The diner is everybody's kitchen.

Diners are a reflection of nostalgia and a step into the American dream. Like the old country store in the center of town, everyone knew that it was a place of family gatherings—of friends and neighbors; white-collar businessmen would have lunch with the blue-collar workers. We might say that it is a place of practicality where the hallmarks are friendly prices, quick service and very fine food. Diners are comfortable, unpretentious and tolerant places where nobody cares where you came from.

Cooks and diner owners considered their kitchens to be their second home. These diners became fashionable, marketable, stylish, and very chic. Many cities and towns featured the diner as an icon with pride equal to the old country store.

Let us treat ourselves to the nostalgia of the roadside eatery—slurp the joe, wolf the waffles, converse with the counter crew. Your neighborhood diner is more than a home away from home; it is an idealized part of America. It was recorded in the *American Heritage Magazine*, April 1977, about the beginning of the diners:

> The diner first appeared, in the form of a lunch wagon, on the streets of Providence, Rhode Island in 1872. In that era, every restaurant in town closed at 8 p.m. It occurred to Walter Scott, a man whose entire previous experience as a restaurateur had been confined to selling pies from a basket, to load a covered express wagon with food and park it outside the offices of the Providence Journal. And there he stayed, every night from dusk until two in the morning, for the next forty-five years, selling sandwiches and boiled eggs to the compositors for a nickel, and sliced chicken to the 'dude trade' for thirty cents.

This eatery idea soon spread and, a decade later, he was imitated with elaborate wagons, kitchens and counters including some with stained-glass windows. The diners began to change: from moving wagons during the late 1800s, to old abandoned street-railroad cars bought for as little as ten dollars each and moved to vacant lots, adding booths, counters and stools for the comfort of their customers. Within a very short time, hundreds of trolley-lunches appeared. The vacant lots were not always glamorous and respectable people did not frequent diners. The question at that time was: how can we legitimize the diner business? This question will be answered in the following chapters. We will witness the classic diners grow, thrive, and become celebrated in our culture. The revival, expansion, and the rebirth of the past are on the horizon.

Our time-capsule of the classic diners of New Hampshire will pass through the turn of the century to the early 1900s; the luster of those "flapper" years when all was "jazz," to the time that Wall Street laid an egg—October 1929; the Deco-craze and the drive-ins, to the 1930s and 1940s; World War II to the age of fast food and restaurant chains.

Decades have passed and the decline of the diner is once again present. Again, like the old country store, competition has put a strain on the industry. However, a revival is in sight, as the public recalls the romance of those golden days of railroad diners—Gilley's Lunch Wagon in Portsmouth, the Littleton Diner, The Red Arrow in Manchester, and the old country store.

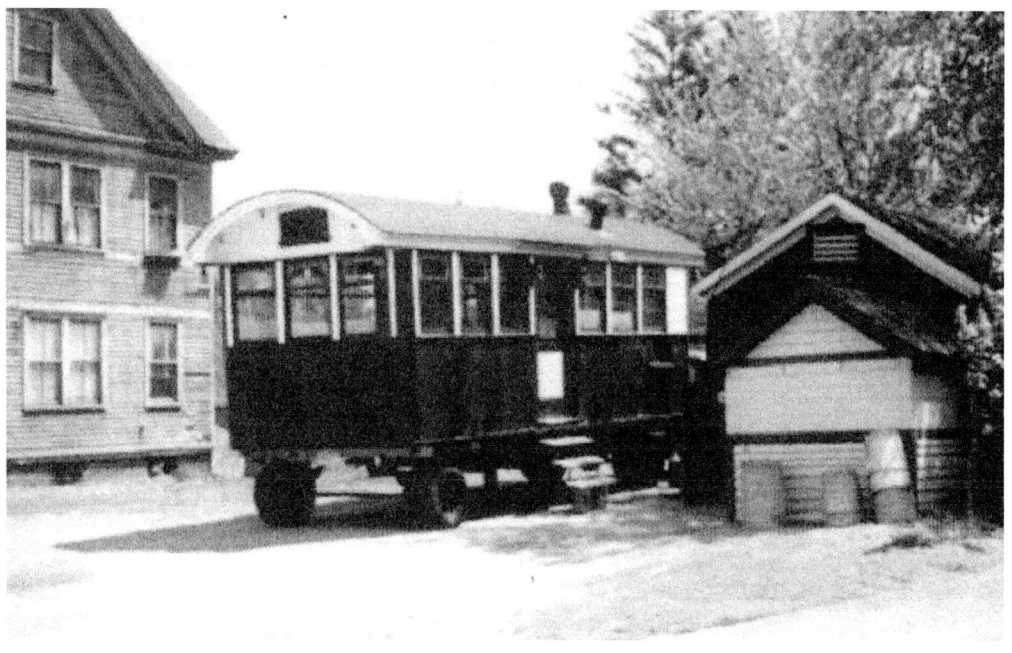

Early Lunch wagon possibly known as Gilley's PM Lunch Wagon, Market Street Portsmouth, NH.
Photo courtesy of Strawbery Banke Museum, Portsmouth

Chapter One

The Origin of the New Hampshire Diners 1872 to 1930s

Originally, the first diners were prefabricated structures built as food wagons and transported to busy locations to serve prepared food to the public. *Webster's Dictionary* defined a diner as "a restaurant in the shape of a railroad car." The word "diner" was derived from the railroad diner and the design reflected the styling that the manufacturers borrowed from the railroad—the Pullman dinner car. The diners at the turn of the twentieth century were outfitted with a counter, stools and a food preparation or service area along the rear wall of the car.

The beginning of the diner car may be traced to Walter Scott (1858), a part-time pressman and type compositor from Providence, Rhode Island. To supplement his income, he decided to sell food, coffee, and sandwiches out of a horse-drawn wagon (Sawyer). He sold to night workers and patrons of evening men's clubs. By the year of 1872, he quit his day job and began selling from his new express wagon parked outside the Providence newspaper office. The first diner with walk-up windows was located on each side of the wagon.

Later these wagons expanded their service by converting to larger wagons, which allowed customers to stand inside, and offered stools at the counter. Historians called these night lunch wagons "Night Owls." These portable wagons became so popular that they began appearing in many New Hampshire towns during the late 1800s. Like many of the Gypsy wagons, they became fitted with colorful glass windows, intricate murals and fancy woodwork—they were most attractive and drew attention from the public. These wagons began to lure workers and pedestrians to the wagon, for the food was good and service fast. The night trade was especially busy, as most eating places closed by 8:00 p.m.

Business was swift and diners attracted many customers; the lunch wagon vendors became as abundant as fast food wagons on the streets; many towns had to pass ordinances in order to restrict their operation. Soon the lunch wagons became so popular that the horse-drawn streetcars (S&R) were becoming obsolete and were replaced with more modern electrified cars. Many unused train cars (diners) were purchased and converted into dining cars. These restored cars lost some of their popularity in many communities.

The image of the diner turned negative as lunch wagons, which were custom built for eating, were replaced by old trolley cars. These cheap cars were located in rough neighborhoods; poor lighting, small windows and dark interiors rightfully gave them the name "greasy spoon." Their appearance, which led the public to shy away from the diner, discouraged the family business.

Once the wheels came off, the cars' change in location made a big difference—their popularity rose dramatically. Diner manufacturing pioneer, Jerry O'Mahony wrote, "In hundreds of cities, locations are waiting for some enterprising businessman or woman. With automobile tourist traffic and freight hauling as heavy as it is today, there are locations on the main turnpikes, near garages or gasoline stations." The Tierney handbook for prospective customers, also stated, "Experience has shown ... the most profitable locations are those where there is 24 hour a day business." In all cases, Tierney and O'Mahony promised to help the new owners of the diners to find a good location before they sold their diners.

The business was so poor that they knew they had to clean up their image, so they added shrubs and flower boxes, added booth service inside the car, and put on a fresh coat of paint to make their diners more respectable. To add a touch of class, the diners added the word "Miss" to their name like "Miss Wakefield's Diner" to help feminize the diner's image.

The diners took on a flavor of class with the construction of special "Lunch Cars" which added indoor rest rooms, long car-length counters with stools, and booths for a party of four to enjoy their favorite meal. These new dining cars of the 1920s and 1930s were extremely well received, but kept the atmosphere of the early lunch wagon.

One of the major lunch car manufacturers was the Worcester Lunch Car Company, which built prefabricated diners and shipped them all over the Eastern Seaboard. The company began building these cars in 1906 with Philip and Irving Stoddard. During the turn of the century, many of these Worcester Car Diners were serving downtown areas without the need to invest in high-priced real estate.

Of note, it is generally accepted that the name "diner" as opposed to "lunch wagon" was not widely used before 1925. Many of these Worcester Diners may still be found in New Hampshire—you would recognize them for they are "classic" in style.

Another popular diner car was created by the Jerry O'Mahony Diner Company. According to Historian Barbara Westergaard, "A Bayonne, New Jersey man by the name of Jerry O'Mahony is credited by some to have made the first diner."

Trade publications record the following: "The Jerry O'Mahony Diner Company of Elizabeth, New Jersey, produced 2,000 diners from 1917 to 1952. Only approximately twenty O'Mahony diners are still in existence throughout the United States" A fine example of the O'Mahony diner may be located on Rte. 25 in Rumney, NH, named "Plain Jane."

Like mobile homes, the style of the diners was and still is rather narrow and elongated and allowed the mobility of roadway transportation from one location to another. You may consider this to be a reflection of the first diners ever built, which were never intended to remain stationary. These original diners, as opposed to the wagons, were considered dining cars on railways. As mentioned earlier, when train dining cars were no longer fit for service, it became useful to convert these cars and create a cheap restaurant located near a train station or along the side of a busy road in the country or suburbs. Modern materials were now being converted into fabricated streamline forms to resemble speed and mobility. The design became identified with the new futuristic mode of transportation—the efficiency of the machine age.

As these diners became more popular, along with the demand to enlarge them, prefabricated cars were being built so as to increase the diner seating space. Like the older lunch wagons, the stationary diner allowed one to set up limited food service using pre-assembled and portable equipment.

Before the Great Depression, most of the manufactured diners were located in the Northeast. During the depression years, the industry of diner manufacturing was limited, however, the service lived on, for people had to eat and the diner offered less expensive meals as compared to the restaurant business. The diner survived and, after the Second World War, our economy improved and the diners returned to expand in the suburbs.

Chapter Two
The Classic Diner Era
1940s to 1980s

This new concept of the classic diner had captured the attention of artists, authors, movie-makers and the general public. The new image and popularity of the diner had now produced a new era of management, appearance and food that created ambiance for a new clientele—the world-class American.

The classic diner is clearly the influence of the railroad dining car. The diners at this time began to adopt a more modern, railroad-car appearance. The new concept is that of elegance with tasteful landscape carpeting the exterior of the diner. Possibly this transformation may be credited to the old and new diner landscape's location. Steel construction, wrap-around windows, and other details symbolized modern America, and the price of the meal still fit the income of the common man. The streamlined Art-deco design combined with the stainless steel projects the new class as post-war image.

According to historian Joseph T. Manzo, "The new diner restaurant is linked to the past by its location on a former diner site, proprietorship by a former diner operator, and through the continued use of counter space where regular customers can gather for coffee and conversation. Diners have always symbolized the optimism of the working American."

Historically, inexpensive good food and service were the most important ingredients for a successful business. Joseph T. Manzo described the Classic Diner perfectly:

> Breakfast was a particularly delightful time in the diner. A cacophony of sound, smells and sights would start the customer's day. The rattling of cups and the rustling of the newspapers mixed with the chatter of customers, snappy talking waitresses and a manager greeting people provided the background for the diner's food. Add to this scene a cook handling several orders at one time in full view of everyone, the smell of coffee brewing and bacon grilling and a counter lines with executives, construction workers, and truck drivers and you have industrial America starting another busy day.

The key to the success of a diner was the chef who cooked out front. This individual provided a show of culinary artistry for the customers, usually while carrying on a conversation with one or more individuals seated at the counter.

In Laconia there was such a diner called the Shore Diner, on the shore of Paugus Bay. Joseph Manzo described this diner to perfection—the entertainment, food, service, and general atmosphere spelled Shore Diner. There was a cook, waiter and entertainer all in one person—the customers called him "Spider."

Sometimes, the local humor might be a little off-color. It was an approach that involved an exchange of insults between the management and the customer. This type of insulting conversation may go on for quite a spell; however, no harm was intended, as the boss was a friend of the regular customer.

Building and personalizing the business was a skill which resulted in success. Building and keeping the clientele was most important—meet the public!

A revival began during the late 1970s. New England hot spots for diner history lovers included Worcester, Massachusetts, the home of the former Worcester lunch Car Company.

The clientele in New Hampshire diners were, and still are, classic and represent a slice of Americana. They served an area with industrial workers who were looking for a quick, cheap meal.

The diner maintains many of its traditions, but it also adjusted to meet the needs of a changing clientele. Its menu is greatly diversified and many diner cars have changed their façade—possibly added brick or wooded over to meet contemporary tastes. However, in New Hampshire one-fourth of the classic diners are still here.

Too many diners are leaving the neighborhood, and the landscape of the small town is changing. The diners continue to lose their share of their market to the fast food establishment. Like the old country store, the larger food establishments and chains are shifting. Everyone is in a hurry. The few remaining diner manufacturers responded to this threat by marketing the diner-restaurant with the Mediterranean style, or the Tudor, and Neoclassical. The American Diner Museum might describe the new façade of the diner as artificial stonework, dark stained wood, earth tone colors, and fabric, which replaced the flashy look of stainless steel, neon, and bold colors. Many of the old diners were remodeled and covered with brick walls and mansard roofs.

Is it possible that we are entering a Renaissance which may spurn a new interest in the American diner? Are there new diner builders who are beginning to fabricate new images of the old diner? New companies may be joining the growing and changing market to produce a new retro-looking diner .

According to the American Diner Museum:

> The renewed interest in diners may be attributed to Americans looking backwards for inspiration and the values of yesterday in a time of moral and economic uncertainty. Several national corporate franchises such as Denny's Silver Diner, and Johnny Rockets adapted the look and feel of the diner as part of new marketing concepts. A trend in diner restaurants developed in Europe that brought increased sales to American diner manufacturers.

Here in New Hampshire I am witnessing a revival of the old classic diner. A significant number of vintage diners have been rescued from demolition and relocated on new sites or have revived the now existing diners in the cities. Surely, a new experience in American diners has been restored.

Manufacturers of the diner structures have experienced a rebirth; new orders or remodeling projects are becoming more prevalent. Historic preservation societies have been placing some vintage functioning diners on the National Register of Historic places. In saving the diner, it is important to help preserve and promote the diner culture. Let us not forget that the diners evolved into a community—a gathering place where people of all walks of life congregated and shared a home-cooked meal as a family in a relaxed atmosphere.

The American diners have become the icon of the American landscape for over 100 years. The influence of lunch wagons and diners has touched many people from all walks of life.

Chapter Three
Cultural Significance and Marketplace

Cultural Significance

Historically, the local diners linked the corner saloons and the fast food restaurants. These institutions bridged the transition from a localized, socially fragmented culture to a mass culture dominated by national and multinational corporations.

The spread of the New Hampshire diners meant that it was possible to cast this institution as a growing symbol of optimism, particularly during the 1940s.

Blue-collar working families rarely took meals away from the home unless they absolutely had to for most of the first half of the twentieth century. The diner created a middle ground between the elegant restaurants and the "greasy spoons" that catered to the lower economic social class.

The neighborhood diners catered to the working-class institutions, and were anchored in a culture that was considered ethnical. Customers were immigrants or second-generation American; German, Italian, Greek and Jewish families dominated the business. Ethnic affiliations did much to build the diner business, and the patrons remained loyal to the class around which the diners had their appeal. However, the clientele was mainly male-oriented working class. These men gathered at the local diners for their entertainment and relaxed leisure time and bantered about sports, politics and work. It was not uncommon to witness coarse language and heavy food, which accounted for much of the diner's popularity among the men.

The all-night diner became a refuge for some undesirable clientele and made the local diner a regular place to elicit their business. Needless to say, many customers believed all diners were just rest stops strictly for a male clientele.

Such clientele deterred the female customers, regardless of their class background. However, during the 1920s and '30s, "flappers" frequently patronized the lunch wagon which often stayed open after the local speakeasies closed.

A change in the traditional diner's marketing was necessary, for they were in danger of losing customers. Manufacturers of diners and new energetic and creative owners began to search for alternative locations and customers.

Many new diner customers were women who had entered the full-time labor force as office workers, retail clerks, and machine operators. With new locations, which drew families, many of the proprietors were attracting a more diversified clientele as compared to the pre-war years. According to Mike Flynn in his article, "I Just Got Back from Lunch," *Diner* (September 1946):

In addition to ladling goulash for hungry laborers and pouring coffee for tired truckers, countermen found themselves frying scrambled eggs for executives on their way to work, preparing sandwiches for female clerical workers on lunch breaks, and slicing pie for couples streaming out of nightclubs and movie theaters. Industry leaders were confident that if they took appropriate steps, they could continue to broaden the constituency, making inroads into a largely untapped market of businessmen, high school kids, young couples, and middle-income families.

New proprietors of local diners had to make creative decisions concerning what to feature as specials and what to add. This would serve as a test for owners as to how far consumers might venture across cultural and social borders. As the clientele changed, so the strategy had to adapt and expand across these borders. This led to the question: how they would repackage the diner as a middle-income family restaurant? Business became better when the clientele trade changed—families replaced workingmen. Proprietors went to extensive lengths to attract more families and to secure more patronage of ladies and children by making the atmosphere and the décor more pleasant, comfortable, and respectable. Indeed this worked; it upgraded the social cachet of eating in a diner.

New Hampshire diners serve American food such as hamburgers, club sandwiches and French fries. Much of the food was grilled, which the early diners had made famous. There was often an emphasis on breakfast, such as eggs, waffles, pancakes and French toast. It is quite common in the diners of today to have the desserts on display in a glass-enclosed pie case. Of note, Northeast shore diners have more of a focus on seafood, such as fried clams and fried shrimp.

First, the proprietors had to lure families out of their homes and kitchens during meal time. With the change of clientele, women were attracted to the food service business at fast food restaurants—women at the counters and men in the back kitchens. The next step for diners was to change the menu by announcing family dinner specials—"A Blue Plate Special."

Andrew Hurley stated in "From Hash House to Family Restaurant: The Transformation of the Diner and Post-World War I Consumer Culture" (*The Journal of American History*, March 1997), "These appeals rested on the assumption that temporary relief from domestic duties would prove attractive to women, especially to the growing numbers of wives who held part- or full-time jobs during the 1950s to help finance families' expanding consumer budgets."

It was not only the women who welcomed dining out—it offered an opportunity for the whole family to bond in a different social environment. Kathy Corbett's June 1995 interview in *American Restaurant Magazine* entitled "Why Do We Eat Out?" referred to the findings of a 1959 study that showed a "scenario played out where the wives were twice as likely as their husbands to suggest that the family eat a meal away from home."

During the 1950s and '60s, proprietors also recognized that the teenage market was a lucrative one, and the installation of jukeboxes and soda fountains testified to the owner's interest in capturing that clientele.

The Marketplace

As time passed, decisions had to be made about the changes that diners were faced with. What do you keep, and what would have to change in order to appeal to a changing clientele?

Now was the time for the entrepreneurs to create a new strategy that the industry would follow to expand across social and cultural borders, and to repackage the diner to meet the needs of progressive tourists and middle-class traveling families.

The industry went to extraordinary lengths to attract these traveling and mobile families—to make their experiences in eating at the diners pleasant, enjoyable, and more comfortable than years past.

During the 1950s, diners faced increasing competition. The significance of the diner's transformation can be better appreciated in the context of our changing commercial dining industry. As restaurants with different historical origins converged on the middle-income family market, the diner industry had to conform, modernize and adapt in order to compete with Howard Johnson, Burger King, and McDonald's, coffee shops, drive-ins and other fast food industrial franchises. These fast-food outlets shared many characteristics with the diner, and these similarities intensified as the proprietors adopted more progressive strategies to deal with competition.

Historian Stuart Ewan's "Captain of Consciousness," records the following: "Something as prosaic as eating lunch has rarely been considered important by historians. Since the early 1970s, historians have studied the attempts of advertising, retailing, and media moguls to manipulate consumer desires."

Chapter Four
Manufacturing the Classic Car Diners
Construction, Style and Design

It is recorded that approximately twelve companies manufactured and sold prefabricated diners during the post-Second World War years (late 1940s). Even though each company advertised its own type of model, the diners constructed at that time exhibited a distinct similarity to each other.

Earlier we mentioned that at the turn of the century, the lunch cars became stationary so as to accommodate more cooking facilities, and that location was of the greatest importance due to the blue collar industrial labor clientele.

The Worcester Lunch Car Company was an early manufacturer of diners based in Worcester, Massachusetts, from 1906 to 1957. The Worcester Car Company produced more than six hundred diners, many of which may be found in New Hampshire. These cars were some of the warmest-looking diners built.

According to historians Donald Kaplin and Alan Bellink in their 1986 publication, *Classic Diners of the Northeast*:

> The construction process was a layered one, starting with a rectangular steel form. Different teams of laborers applied their skill to the essential structure. First was the interior crew, who filled the frame with twenty-gauge steel. Electrical and plumbing work was next, followed by oak or mahogany paneling for the walls. The masonry was done by an Italian crew, who showed an amazing amount of care for detail in the hand-tiled mosaic floors and counter base. After the cooking equipment was installed, large sheets of porcelain enamel were layered on the exterior.

The Jerry O'Mahony Diner Company of Elizabeth, New Jersey, as recorded by historian Karen Offitzer, "became the largest manufacturer of the period." Having built its first lunch car in 1913, it was considered one of the oldest manufacturers in the nation, and produced approximately two thousand diners until 1941. Many of these O'Mahony roadside diners are long, narrow, and mostly metal buildings which were prefabricated in the New Jersey factory. There were at least twenty-six pre-war Streamline Modern style O'Mahony diners built between 1932 and 1941. A fine example of the O'Mahony diner is Plain Jane Diner located on Route 25 in Rumney, New Hampshire.

During the period of Prohibition (1920–1933), the diners prospered greatly since the competition of the local saloon was eliminated. By the 1940s, the new face of the classic cars had carved out their place in the food industry and became a familiar attraction in the factory scene.

When the Second World War had ended, most of the diner industry continued to fulfill their established function of serving inexpensive but hearty food to the labor class. With no formal background in design, the manufacturers drew upon the familiar and the comfortable: the family kitchen, the parlor, and the trolley and railroad cars. The industry took what they saw around them in order to create the diner's feeling of warmth. The construction of the new style of diner was to provide a larger working and customer space. However, few dining cars exceeded fifty feet in length and seventeen in width. The basic interior featured a long counter in front of a row of closely-knit stools, with booths and tables lined against the front wall, which were tightly packed next to the windows. The manufacturers placed the cooking facilities directly behind the counter in order to expedite service so there was no need to hire waiters or waitresses to carry most of the food except to table service. With this style of interior design, menus were not needed—a large signboard with the menu of specials was displayed above the grill so the customers made their selections from the board.

When the 1950s arrived, many diner manufacturers were producing about twenty-five new diners each year. The new image of the diner made its way into suburban shopping centers, seaside resorts, and small college towns, such as the Main Street Diner in Plymouth, New Hampshire, which catered to the college students.

In 1955, the Cullman Dining Car Company announced "the newest idea since diners began... the Kullman Drive-in Diner." This would offer another model—the "diner-restaurant"—which would feature a waiting area, a larger dining room, and a kitchen equipped for a "complete restaurant menu." A good example of this style of diner is Miss Caron's Diner in Hillsborough, New Hampshire.

By 1956, the Mountain View Diners, manufactured in New Jersey, boasted that they had diners which covered the territory from the Atlantic to the Mississippi River. Mr. Petropouleas, owner of the company, said the following:

> I consider diners the people's restaurant. You can accommodate everyone, from the poor to the wealthy. Someone can come wearing a tux and order Surf & Turf. You can also come in wearing shorts and order a hotdog or coffee and dessert. However, most diner manufacturers remained with the more distinctive and conservative style, which directed their business to the customer familiar to the traditional diners.

At this time, new diners appeared in what we might call "white-collar" areas. It was not uncommon to see these new classic diners in areas where you could find second- and third-generation Americans who had leaped the collar line. This is when the proprietors relayed shifting consumer taste to the builders, leading to an evolution in diner architecture—visual appeal.

Locations of diners might be on busy highways (truck stops), such as the Tilt'n Diner which is off an I-93 exit, or at other intersections like the Roundabout Diner in Portsmouth. Other popular locations could be found in Manchester at the Red Arrow Diner; Laconia at the Union Diner; Main Street in Littleton at the Littleton Diner; Route 16 in Sanbornville at the Miss Wakefield; or Portsmouth at Gilley's Wagon Diner, to name a few.

To handle the increasing volume of customers, many new owners of diners added separate dining rooms to the rear of the diner car so as not to change the appearance of the classic diner. The builders furnished their dining room annexes with knotty-pine wall panels which bore a striking resemblance to that of Howard Johnson's wall design. Several diners throughout the state car companies improved their business because they annexed their rear dining room to accommodate their volume of a growing clientele. Eventually, manufacturers delivered diners that measured two thousand square feet and seated more than one hundred guests at a time; many of them provided privacy for the family-sized booths.

Jerry O'Mahony Car Company announced that it would equip its cars with mirrored ceilings in order to create the impression of space and a luxurious atmosphere. The company also changed the color scheme by offering pastel colors for a "brighter and richer appearance, as well as for their psychological effect." The move was very effective, for other companies soon followed suit.

In addition to these drastic changes, the proprietors tried to provide a pleasurable and comfortable dining experience by providing air conditioners. Perhaps the most dramatic change made by the diner industry was to move the grill from behind the counter to a separate kitchen behind the diner. By placing all the cooking facilities in the rear kitchen, it removed the griddle man and his greasy operation from the customers' view. With the new space, came booth seating, lighter fares, redecorated interior and increased table service. By retaining the counter, proprietors were still able to serve a predominantly male clientele.

Diners were now providing a spacious parking area and a bright, original neon sign next the road entrance to draw the customer to their more attractive diner. At this time, you could easily find a diner near an airport, shopping mall, sports arena, motel, or seaside resort.

Historian-authors, Max Boas and Steve Chain, have put this rebirth of the diner in its proper perspective, in *Smithsonian*, November 1986:

> Diners may have paved the way for the triumph of the local diner; their fast service, rock-bottom prices, informality, and attention to the needs of families enables the fast-food chains to replicate much of what diners offered with even greater consistency and without any traces of a working-class linage. Standardizing food and service in addition to architecture, they offered an experience that was acceptable and familiar to patrons of diverse class backgrounds and, above all, identical from Maine to California. By introducing many Americans to this type of consumer experience, diner owners may have sowed the seed of their own demise.

Since the 1980s, New Hampshire has renewed its love affair with the great American diners. The general public and tourists have gained much by rediscovering the special heritage and nature of these roadside classic diners. New Hampshire's "diner entrepreneurs" are witnessing a revival for the classical diners and old country stores, and have seen a renaissance of the railroads' tourist business. This renewed appreciation has changed the State's tourist industry.

A List of American Diner Builders was written by Marybeth Shanahan who wishes to share the origin, nostalgia, and manufacturing information of the original companies in America. Marybeth is the proprietor of the Dream Diner of Tyngsboro, MA, and has named the Diners' omelets after the manufacturers. According to Marybeth, this is: "a tribute to the great American success story, not only in the basic formulas of hard work and long hours, but the appreciation of customers."

These are the major manufacturers of the classic diners in America, according to Marybeth Shanahan:

Wilfred H. Barriere. Worcester, MA. 1905–1906, 1926–1930. Barriere built diners of various sizes until 1930.

Bixler Manufacturing Company. Norwalk, OH. 1931–1937? Bixler diners featured large width, two-foot double hung windows and a barrel roof.

Bramson Engineering Company. Oyster Bay, NY. During the mid-1950s. Bramson started building diners as a sideline with one still extant as the Aero Diner in Connecticut.

J. G. Brill Company, Dining Car Division. Philadelphia, PA. 1927–1932. Brill was a noted manufacturer of street railway vehicles when in 1927, they introduced a line of all-steel diners. Note: The Capitol Diner of Lynn, MA is a surviving example from this company.

T. H. Buskley Lunch Wagon Mfg. Worcester, MA. 1891–1908. Thomas H. Buckley became the first "Lunch Wagon King", setting up wagons in some 250 towns throughout the country.

Campora Dining Car Company. Kearny, NJ. 1957. This short-lived company was started by Jerry Campora, a former shop supervisor at the Killman Diners. The company may have only built one diner.

Comac, Inc. Irvington, NJ. 1947–1951. Two Comac-built diners still in existence are Tastee Diner of Laurel, Maryland, and Jack's Diner of Albany, NY.

DeRaffele Manufacturing Company, Inc. New Rochelle, NY. 1933–Present. In 1921, Angelo DeRaffele started out as a carpenter, advancing in 1927 to the position of foreman at P. J. Tierney Sons. In 1933, DeRaffele began to manufacture diners at the old Tierney plant. In 1947, DeRaffele was joined by his son Philip after the Second World War. DeRaffele is currently known as the largest manufacturer of diners.

Diner-Mite Diners. Atlanta, GA. 1959–Present. This company has been building modular food-service units of varying shapes and sizes under names such as Module Mobile, Inc. and Diner Group Limited.

Erfed Corporation. Rutherford, NJ., 1956–mid-1970s. Started by Erwin Fedkenheuer, Sr., the former lead sheet-metal man with Paramount Diners for nearly 20 years prior. Along with his son Erwin Junior, and several other sheet-metal workers from Paramount, the company specialized in the repair, modernization and renovation of existing diners on location.

Fodero Dining Car Company. Bloomfield, NJ. 1933–1981. Joseph Fodero started out at P. J. Tierney Sons in 1922 and later worked for Kullman before starting his own company in 1933. Fodero built some of the more stylish designs in the industry and is noted for its famous winged clock.

Galion Diners. Galion, OH? Little is known of this company. The Penn Yan Diner of Penn Yan, NY, was reportedly built by Galion.

John J. E. Hennigan. Worcester, MA. 1907–1917. First operating a night lunch wagon in 1899 in Worcester, Hennigan started manufacturing in 1907, building a model known as the Franklin Lunch Wagon.

Kullman Dining Car Company. Lebanon, NJ. 1927–Present. Founded in 1927 by Samuel Kullman, the former accountant for P. J. Tierney Sons. Starting out in Newark, the firm subsequently relocated to Harrison, NJ, and then on to Avenel, NJ, prior to moving to their current state-of-the-art facility in Lebanon. Samuel's grandson Robert became president of the company, which has always built a high-quality diner. His company (presently known as Kullman Industries) also builds modular buildings for uses as U.S. Embassies, schools, prison facilities and bank buildings.

Manno Dining Car Company. Fairfield, NJ. 1949–1978. The company was founded in 1949 by Ralph Manno and Vincent Giannotti, both formerly with Kullman Diners. Starting out as a diner renovating company, they went on to build various styles of diners including all brick exterior "colonial" diners and some unusual examples with nearly all-glass façades and interesting stainless steel work.

Master Diners. Pequannock, NJ. 1947–mid-1950s. Master was a small company that built stainless steel diners in two or three styles and various sizes. The Sunny Day Diner of Lincoln, NH, is a small Master Diner.

Mountain View Diners. Singac, NJ. 1939–1957. This company outsold most all of the other manufacturers in the 1950s with an aggressive marketing campaign, sending their units all over the country. While attempting to go public in June 1956, the company foundered and went out of business shortly thereafter.

Mulholland Company. Dunkirk, NY. 1920–1930? Founded as the Mulholland Spring Company in 1881, this company evolved over the years building a full line of buggies, carriages, and road wagons advancing to automobiles, trucks, and ambulance bodies. Around 1920 they branched out into diner manufacturing.

Musi Dining Car Company. Carteret, NJ. 1966–Present. Formerly with Kullman Dining Car Company, Ralph Musi started his own company in 1966, building new diners in the Colonial and Mediterranean styles.

Jerry O'Mahony. Elizabeth, NJ. 1913–1956. Jerry O'Mahony (1890–1969) was the creator of the Jersey Diner. He sold port and beans and corned beef hash from horse-drawn lunch wagons in Bayonne, then later bought stationary cars, which he renamed diners. By 1929, O'Mahony and his brother, Sam, were among to top three producers of the lunch cars. At the start of the twentieth century, diners began to be prefabricated—mostly in New England and in New Jersey—and delivered ready to start dishing it out. During the days of the flappers, diner manufacturers deliberately began mimicking the look of railroad dining cars to add a little "class" to their products. Oh, you kids! Nothing was more elegant than traveling by train in those days. (*History—"A step back in time"*)

Orleans Manufacturing Company. Albion, NY. 1947–1948. Orleans only built three diners: The Cadillac Diner of Westwood, NJ, the Arlington Diner of Haverhill, MA, and the Dauphin's Superior Diner of Rochester, NY. Dauphin's is still operating today as the Highland Park Diner on its original location.

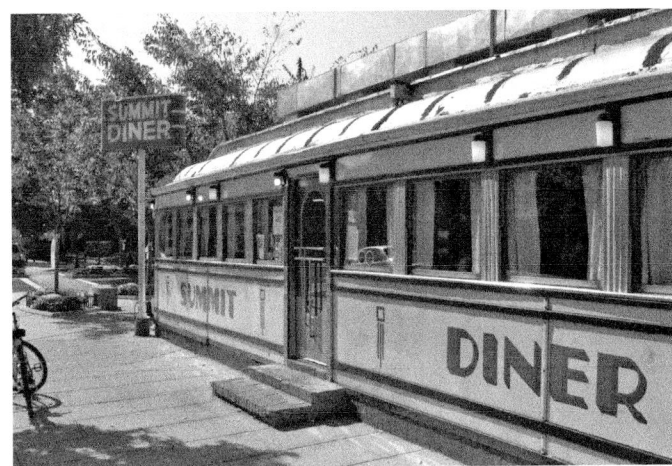

A classic O'Mahony Diner. A prototypical "rail car" style diner, built by the O'Mahony Company in 1938. This particular example is in New Jersey.

Charles H. Palmer. Worcester, MA. 1889–1901. Charles Palmer was the first to receive the patent for his design for a night lunch wagon. Becoming one of the first early successful wagon builders, his enterprise was ended in 1901 when fire struck his factory in Sterling Junction, Massachusetts.

Paramount Diners. Oakland, NJ. 1932–Present. Known for their stainless steel work on the interior. Paramount offered the all-stainless-steel exterior before anyone else, developed and patented the split-construction method now widely used in the modular building industry.

The Pollard Company. Lowell, MA. 1926–1927. Pollard built a handful of barrel-roofed diners. The Palace Diner of Biddeford, Maine and the Riverside Diner (now Bristol Diner) of Bristol, NH, are the only two survivors from this manufacturer.

Rochester Grills. Rochester, NY. 1940–? There is very little information concerning this manufacturer that built diners in the same style as Bixler.

Silk City Diners (Paterson Vehicle Company). Paterson, NJ. 1927–1964. The Paterson Vehicle Company, which was operated by the Cooper family since 1886, began as wagon builders. They eventually made automobiles, bus and truck bodies before starting to make "Silk City Diners" in 1927. They were the lowest priced diner that you could buy from at the time.

Sorge Diner Manufacturing Company. Silver Creek, NY. Dates of operation unknown. Sorge Brothers was one of several companies that popped up in the Lake Erie region following the success of Ward & Dickinson.

Starlite Diners. Holly Hill, FL. 1992–Present. This company offers a standard diner finished in mirror-finish stainless steel in 14 ft. x 76 ft. units that seat 52 people. They presently build custom units seating upward of 150 people. Starlite has shipped diners all over the world and recently has been building Denny's Classic Diners for the Denny's restaurant chain.

Sterling Diners, (J. B. Judkins Company). Merrimac, MA. 1936–1942. John B. Judkins Company built carriages from 1857–1910, motorcar bodies from 1910–1936 and then entered the diner-building business. The most famous model Sterling built was the streamliner with one or both ends configured in a bullet shape.

Superior Dining Car Company. Berlin, NJ. 1950s. Superior was a diner-renovating company about which very little is known.

Swingle Diners. Middlesex, NJ. 1957–1988. Previously in sales with Fodero and Jerry O'Mahony, Joseph Swingle began his own diner-building operation in August of 1957. In their 31 years of dining building, Swingle completed 147 units. The Victoria Diner still operating on Massachusetts Avenue in Boston's South End is a Swingle Diner.

Patrick J. Tierney. New Rochelle, NY. 1905–1917. "Pop" Tierney operated lunch wagons from 1895 onward and began manufacturing them around 1905 in a small garage behind his home. After his death in 1917, his sons Edward and Edgar took over the business until 1927, renaming it P. J. Tierney Sons, Inc.

Valentine Manufacturing Company. Wichita, KS. 1938–1974. Most of the units were found in the mid-west and west, the rest of the units were shipped to the east coast. The most popular model was known as the "Little Chef", an eight or ten stool one-man operation, with take-out service. They were finished in porcelain enamel or painted steel and featured integral pylon signage.

Ward & Dickinson. Silver Creek, NY. 1923–1940. Charles Ward and Lee F. Dickinson built a distinctive diner based in the designs of railroad or trolley cars. They were considered the most prolific builders of diners in the Lake Erie region of New York.

Worcester Lunch Car Company. Worcester, MA, 1906–1961. Starting with Car Number 200, Worcester built 651 diners. Car Number 850–Lloyd's Diner of Johnston, RI (currently Route 104 Diner, formerly known as Bobby's Girl Diner, of New Hampton, NH) was the last diner off the assembly line in 1957.

Chapter Five

List of Classic Diners in New Hampshire

Airport Diner (C-Man) opened in 2005 and serves the traditional American style menu—good food. The diner is conveniently located near the Manchester-Boston Regional Airport. For your entertainment, the diner is complete with be-boppin' music. The Airport Diner is a family restaurant which offers something for everyone. The Boston Globe called theirs "a local tuna melt worth traveling for."

The Airport diner is located at 2280 Brown Avenue, Manchester, NH 03101.

The Airport Diner brags that:

Whether you take advantage of our hearty breakfasts served all day long, like our popular B-52 Bomber, or our comfort food favorites American Chop Suey and Chicken Pot Pie—just like mom used to make—you're sure to leave Airport Diner satisfied.

Don't forget our classic frappes, flavored Cokes and a slice of our very own pie, topped off with our Common Man-made ice cream.

The Airport Diner is open 24 hours a day. Whether you stop for breakfast, lunch or dinner meal, you'll totally enjoy the service, the fifty's atmosphere, and the homemade meals. A stop at the diner is worthwhile and satisfying.

Public Reviews of the Airport Diner:

November 26, 2012—it was late one night after we arrived in Manchester from our flight from Houston. We were hungry and this was the only place we could find that was open. 'Oh great—this will be wonderful,' I said in my most sarcastic way. I'm a vegetarian and was really not looking forward to diner food.

Walking in it looked like any other diner, maybe a little hipper, but still classic diner. There were several tables full of people and lots of burgers on the griddle. I was still doubtful! We were seated quickly, and greeted by a jolly man, who was quick witted and offered up some great local brews to start!

As I flipped through the menu, there it was—A house-made veggie burger! What, where did they come from? Was I delirious? Nope—it was actually right there on the page in front of me—I ordered the 'veggie melt'. I was blown away by its yumminess. I haven't had a veggie burger that good for years! My friend had one as well and said the same thing!

The other meals the guys had were the tuna melt and beef tips. Both were impressed with the quality of the food.

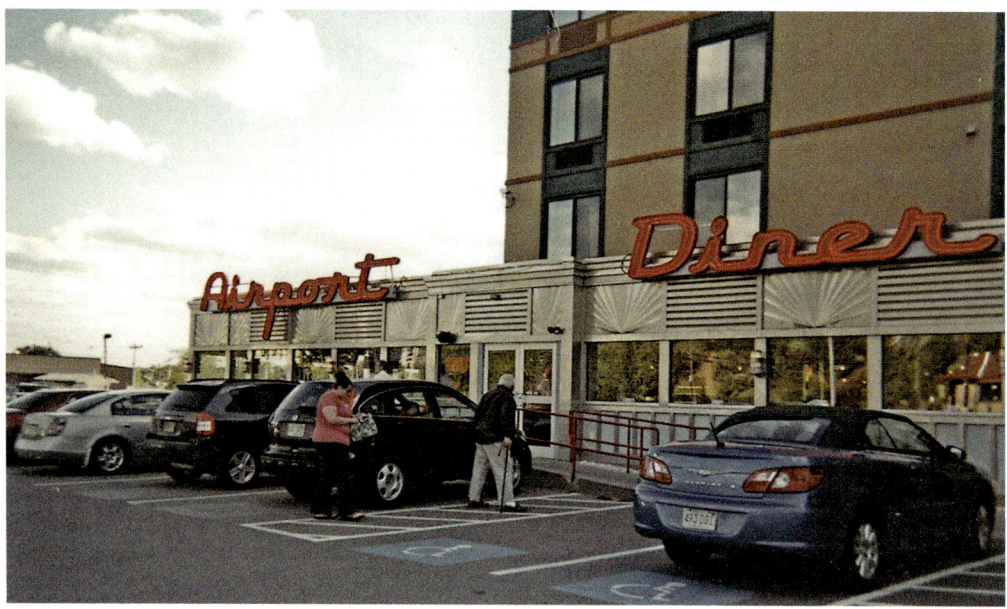

Airport Diner on Brown Street, Manchester, NH. The diner is conveniently located on Brown Street near the Manchester-Boston Airport in Manchester, NH. *Photo courtesy of the author.*

Signed,
Robyn W.
Houston, TX

February 25, 2013—I have been going to the Airport Diner for years and have always had a great time and great service! The staff welcoming and the atmosphere is everything you would want from a retro diner! Their great vintage airplanes are always a hit with my young son!

Signed,
Jodi R.
Manchester, NH

June 25, 2012—Popped in here on a Sunday morning around 11:45. Place was packed, but we didn't have to wait at all for a high top selection was great, prices were awesome and service was on point. I had toast, eggs and hash browns, and my boyfriend had toast, eggs, hash browns, pancakes, sausage and bacon. Silly amounts of food.

   I will definitely go back next time I fly in or out of Manchester!

Signed,
Sarah L.
Arlington, MA

April 20, 2011—Part of the reason I chose to stay in the Holiday Inn next door when I had to travel to Manchester for a work event was due to great Yelp reviews of the Airport Diner.

The food did not disappoint me when I stopped in for dinner on a Saturday night. The bison burger with cheese, sweet potato fries, and strawberry ice cream soda were all tasty.

The staff was friendly and I saw a bunch of families with kids enjoying a meal.

As an added bonus, I saw pin ups of sneakers on the diner walls, supporting the National MS Society, a nonprofit I am a supporter of as well.

Signed,
Danielle K.
Quincy, MA

August 16, 2011—Another Common Man restaurant. This place is great—It's always very clean and the breakfast entrees are tasty (with very large portions.)

Good coffee and the service is usually pretty attractive. Decent shakes. It's on par with their Tilton diner counterpart.

One thing that surprised me was their chicken dinner is (or at least was back when I tried ordering it) based on chicken fingers—not on the bone poultry. Thankfully, the waitress gave me a heads up on this before I finished ordering.

Signed,
Chad H.
Derry, NH

Bristol Diner was built in 1926. It is one of the only two Pollard diners left. The other one is the Palace Diner in Biddeford, Maine. The diner is located at 33 South Main Street at the bridge in Bristol, NH 03222.

Public Reviews of the Bristol Diner:

November 16, 2009—I stopped for lunch at the Bristol Diner (formerly Riverside Diner) recently. This class breakfast & lunch diner was built by the Pollard Company in 1920. The front lunch car portion houses a long counter with stool seating plus attached kitchen and dining room (with a booth seating) sections.

The breakfast menu offerings include eggs, omelets, French toast, pancakes, and breakfast sides. The lunch menu offers grilled & cold sandwiches, burgers, deep fried steak & cheese wrap, quesadillas, hot dogs, chili, salads, chicken tenders, chopped sirloin fried seafood, liver & onions, homemade fries & onion rings, and desserts (pies, cakes). Fresh brewed coffee is from Donahue Bros. and Pepsi fountain drinks. Beer is available including Budweiser, Bud Light, Miller, Miller Light, Michelob, Guinness, Corona. The prices here are fair, all items under $10.00.

I sat at the lunch counter for quick service. I got an ice water and I decided on the BBQ Pulled Pork Sandwich ($5.95) served with chips & dill pickle chips, but I upgraded the chips to homemade

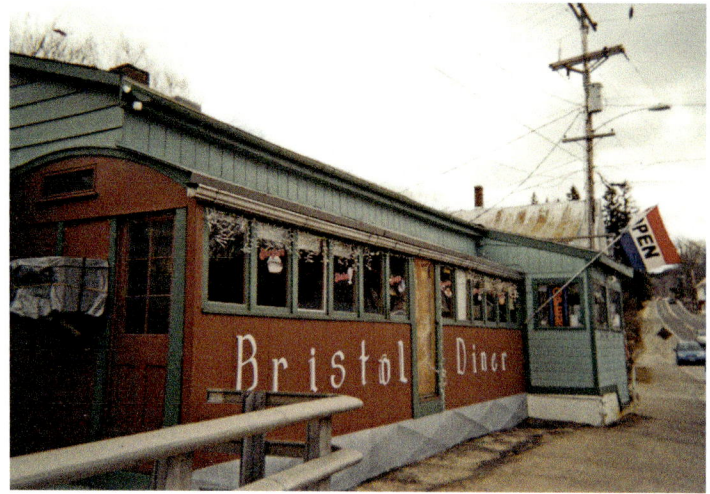

Bristol Diner is a Pollard Diner, built in 1926, and is considered to be one of only two Pollard diners in existence. The diner is located in the village of Bristol, NH. *Photo courtesy of the author.*

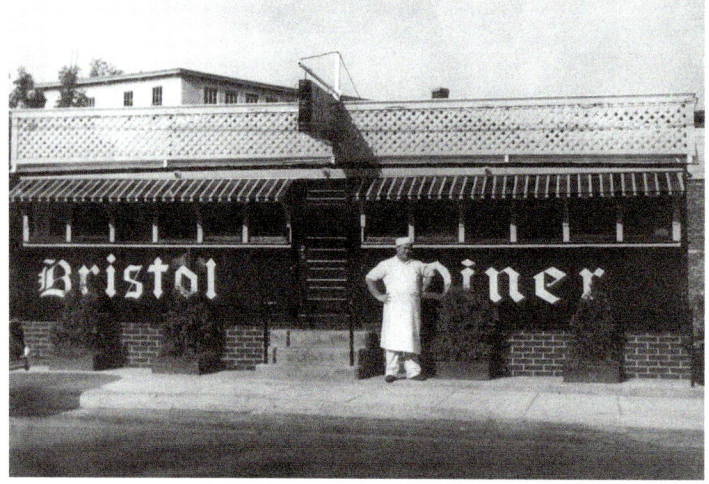

Bristol Diner as seen during the 1950s with the chef posing in front of the diner. (Chef unknown). *Photo courtesy of the Bristol Diner.*

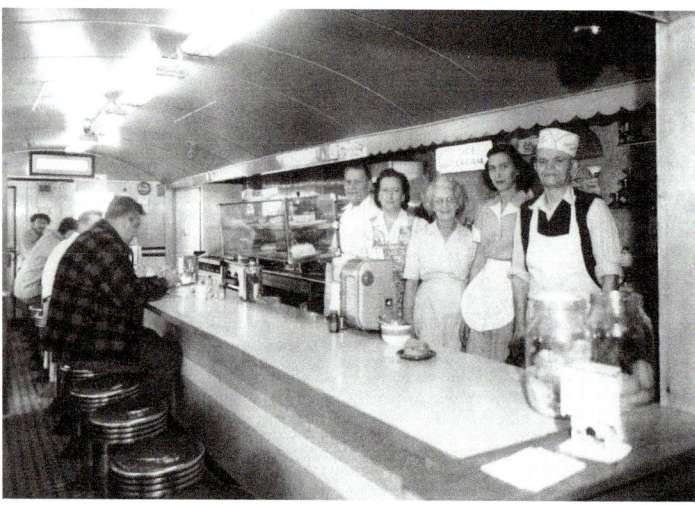

Staff—The Bristol Diner crew proudly poses for the camera. From left to right: Georte Totas, Jessie Holnburn Morgan, Belle Jones, Kay Riley, Jim Pappas and customer at the counter is Aaron Sathero. *Photo courtesy of the Bristol Diner.*

fresh cut shoestring fries (add $1.50). The food was ready in 10 minutes. The big sandwich had tender pulled pork (some fat) with a sweet BBQ sauce and melted cheese on a large soft toasted bulkie roll, pretty decent overall. The hot homemade fries were okay, a bit of a soft texture and not too greasy. The service was attractive and quick.

Signed,
Ian W.
Pelham, NH

Daddy Pops Tumble Inn diner was built in 1941 by the Worcester Diner Company (# 778). The diner is still located at its original location in Claremont. This diner is considered a one-of-a-kind car. According to the owners, the lettering on the diner's side facade is original and unique for Worcester. However, in 1977, the name "Daddy Pop's" was added to the diner's name. The diner serves simple American food—breakfast and lunch only. The diner is located at 1 Main Street, Claremont, NH 03743.

According to author/historian, Randy Garbin:

... the diner has appeared in about every book of diner photographs and paintings published. The diner sit atop a high foundation, and from the street, photographers get an angle that includes the handsome nineteenth-century hotel that looms in the background. Since 1997, the Tumble Inn belonged to Ken Smith of Hatboro, Pennsylvania. People in the town know about his Daddypop's Diner and it reputation for large meals.

During the 1990's the diner passed through four owners. Brenda Rubera, who sold it to Larry Beswick. He sold it to Sue Durfey. After several years, a New Hampshire native by the name of Ken Smith purchased the diner in 1997. Ken in turn gave the operation of the diner over to his daughter Debbie Carter and her husband. The family gave the diner a face-lift and re-opened in 1998 as Daddypop's Tumble Inn.

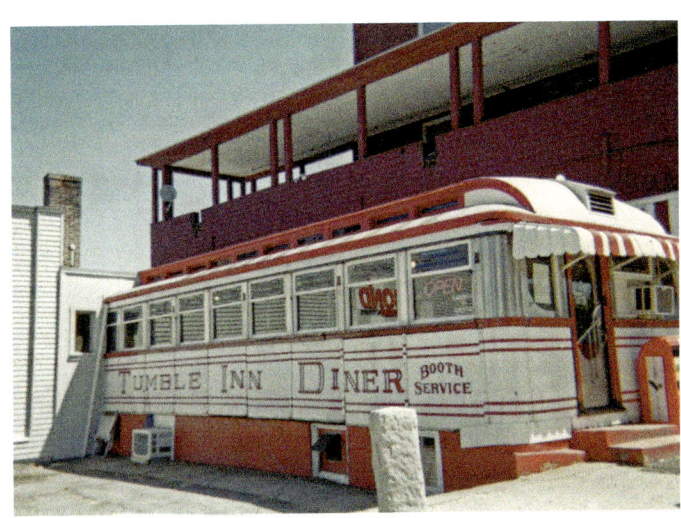

Daddypops Tumble Inn Diner is a 1941 Worcester (#778), located in Claremont, NH. *Photo courtesy of Minette Sweeney and the Daddypop Tumble Inn Diner.*

It was in 2002 that Debbie made the diner smoke-free, which was a positive move for sales increased for more than 15%.

Public Reviews of Daddy Pop's Tumble Inn:

October 3, 2012—I had lunch here today with my wife. It was pretty standard diner fare, though a somewhat limited menu. I had a steak sandwich, and she had a bacon cheeseburger. The décor is just what you'd expect from the 50+ year old railcar converted into a diner—custom-made wooden booths, a long counter...

Signed,
Todd B.

September 3, 2012—had a chance to get out of town for the day Sunday on my motorcycle and I took full advantage of it. After a real nice 165 mile ride, I pulled into Daddy Pops and bellied up to the counter starving and in dire need of some hot coffee pretty quick. You know what I mean, you want and need the first one in...

Signed,
Customer.

March 4, 2007—Ladies and gentlemen: This is a VERY OLD LOCAL DINER! An old diner car just off of the Pleasant Street rotary. Standard diner fare, and a very local crowd. It's like going back to the 1950's, no the 40's. Not sure but decide for yourself. Claremont needs your business.

Signed,
Matthew A.

Fast Eddie's Diner is a classic-style diner typical of the 1950s—classic diner featuring hamburger sandwiches, soup and salads. The 'home style cooked grilled salmon topped with green onions, lemon butter and served with roasted potatoes and sautéed fresh vegetables' is extraordinary.

The diner's printed history reads as follows:

Fast Eddie's Diner was the creation of Eric and Kathleen Rush. In 2003 Kathleen and son Eric converted an old Pizza Hut building into the 50s style diner it is today. They opened the doors March 2004 in the name and honor of Kathleen's deceased husband Ed Houck 'Fast Eddie.' Today Fast Eddie's Diner is open seven days a week serving Breakfast, Lunch & Diner. We like to think our food and service is top notch. All the food is prepared from scratch, including all soup stocks, sauces and salad dressings and the staff is happy to serve it to you and make you feel at home.

Serving traditional and non-traditional diner fare, we are proud of the selection and diversity of food offered in our restaurant. Come in to enjoy the experience and taste the difference. We are the proud recipients of the Best of NH 2007 Best 50s Style Diner!

The diner is located at 320 Lafayette Rd., Hampton, NH 0384.

Four (4) Aces Diner was one of those places where the customers were eager to share their memories with the owner. This 1952 Worcester diner (#837) has a two-story frame building completely enveloping it. In architectural terms, this is a diner travesty, but open the door and the Four Aces reveals a perfect Fifties interior, with counter, stools, grill, and booths. American food is the standard diner fare.

This is where the locals eat. The owners brag that the Four Aces is what a diner should be—totally vintage. The diner recommends the corned beef hash, the fries with melted cheese. To please the appetite, the chef will stuff the pancakes with most anything you request. This is a must visit and enjoy your meal.

The diner is located on 23 Bridge St. (Rt. 4), West Lebanon, NH 03784.

Public Reviews of Four Aces Diner:

January 18, 2013—(from the guest book)—Although I live in the area, I haven't been to the diner for years. I don't know why. My mother and I stopped for lunch. I had the fish and chips and she the turkey dinner. Nothing was greasy or tasted bad. I will be going back there in the very near future.

Signed,
Timothy Pyer

August 12, 2012—(from the guest book)—Continues to be my favorite. We drive quite a distance to go for breakfasts, which are always great. This week we stopped in and one of our favorite waitresses mentioned they were 'trying out' hash browns and which we love their home fries, we decided to try the new offering. My wife and the waitress discussed seasoning (the thing that makes the home fries great) and she offered to have that put on the hash browns. What a GREAT combination, and typical of their willingness to do things for the customer. Definitely worth the drive, every time.

Signed,
Andy Van Abs
Customers

May 22, 2012 (from the guest book)—We were passing through the area on our way back to CT and were so fortunate to have 'stumbled' upon your magnificent diner! This place is super clean and our meals were excellent as was our waitress. We will definitely be return customers when we pass through again!! Many thanks.

Signed,
Leigh & Laura
Customers

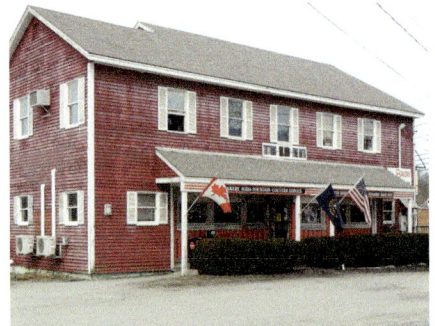
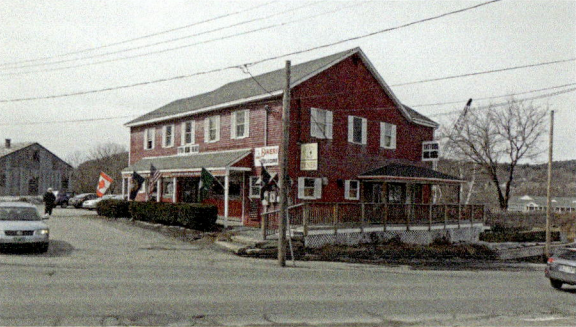
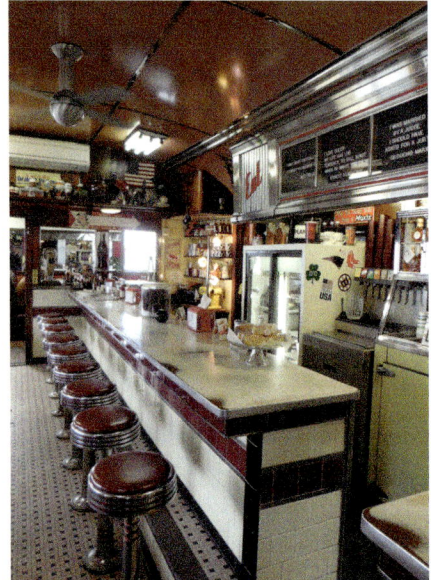
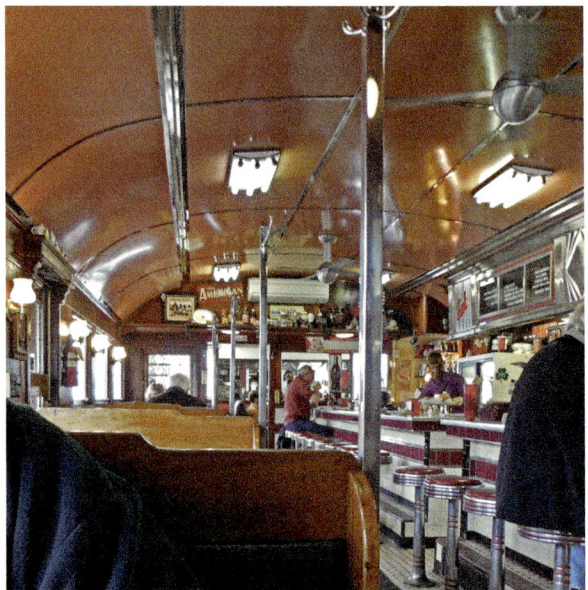
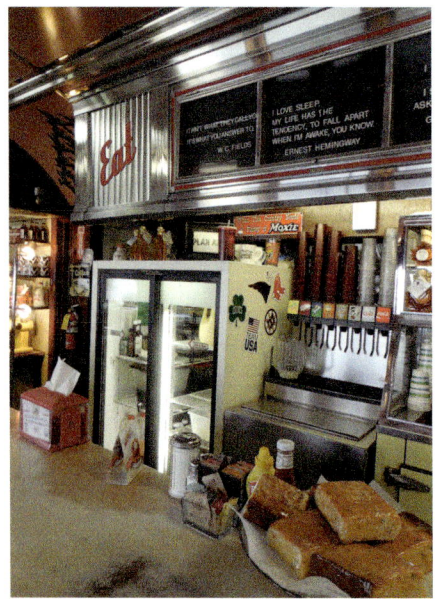
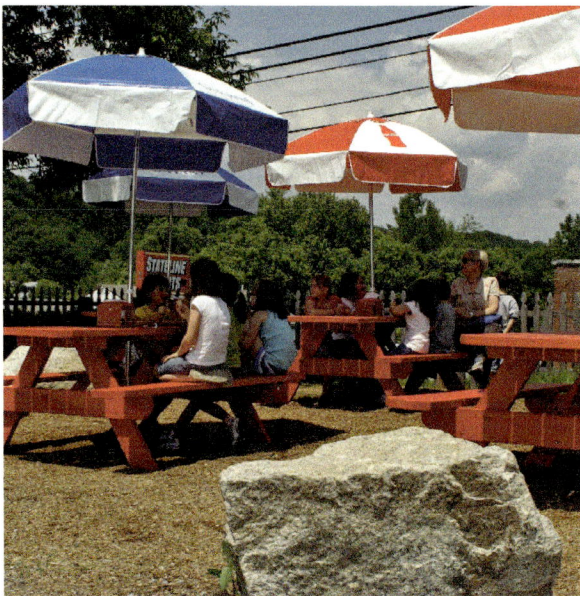

Previous page: Four Aces Diner is a Worcester Diner (#837). *Photos courtesy of Ron Scully*

April 15, 2012 (from the guest book)—I went to the Four Aces Diner for the first time today with two good friends. The food was awesome. The waitress was very attractive and the experience was wonderful. I will go to the Four Aces again and again.

Signed,
Barbara Kendall—Gregory
Customers.

Gilley's PM Lunch Wagon was originally built in 1940 by the Worcester Diner Company of Worcester, Massachusetts. Gilley's Diner is located on 175 Fleet St. in Portsmouth, NH 03801.

According to Stephen and Gina Kennedy, owners of Gilley's Diner, the following history is given:

This diner is one of just five that were built, and is the only one remaining in full operation today.

This diner, and its predecessor, were hauled into Market Square each evening and parked in front of the North Church in preparation for the evening's business. Originally the diner was towed by horse, then tractor and finally by truck. The mural painted by John Perry depicts Gilley's in the 1900s in Market Square. Gilley's was moved to its present location in June 1974.

Although permanently situated, Gilley's retains the same characteristics and authenticity as when it was mobile. The interior contains the original oak, porcelain trim and fixtures. Every effort is made to retain the original charm and character of this historic diner.

Gilley's is named after longtime employee Ralph 'Gilley' Gilbert. Gilley served hot dogs and burgers from the diner's tiny kitchen for over five decades. An icon in Portsmouth history, Gilley was known for his flawless memory, kindness and generosity. He greeted his customers by name, had a good word for everyone and never let the lack of funds prevent a hungry customer from eating. Gilley died in 1986 but his name and fame continues.

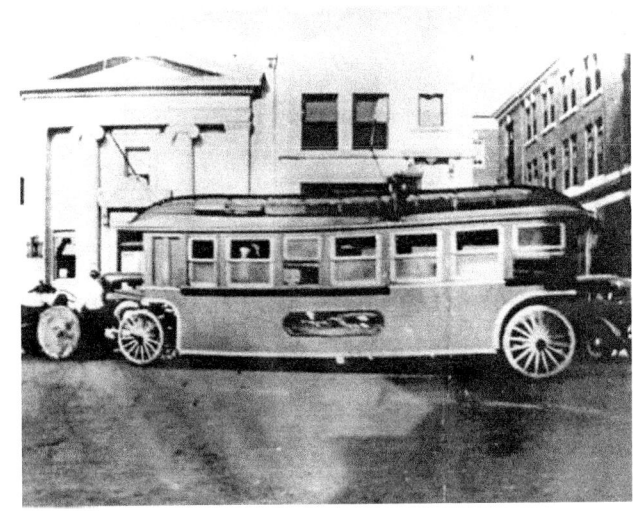

Gilley's diners pulled by truck. Gilley's night-owl lunch wagon (diner) is now permanently set on Fleet Street in Portsmouth, NH. The diner is truly a landmark and legend of Portsmouth. *Courtesy of Stephen and Gina Kennedy.*

The business was established in 1912. According to Gilley's Web site, the lunch cart was built in 1940, by the Worcester Diner Co. of Worcester, Mass. Its last-known improvement was a wing added to the cart on May 1996.

The wing added to Gilley's in May 1996 combined the diner with its former separate storage trailer. In September 2010 that wing was expanded. The additional storage and refrigeration facilities enabled Gilley's to expand its menu, improve safety, security and provide better service to their valued customers.

In is interesting to note that Gilley's Diner is one of only five that were built and is the only one remaining in full operation today. It should also be noted that the truck that towed the diner retains the same characteristics as when it was mobile. Now every effort is made to retain the original charm and character of this historic diner.

For more on history of Gilley's, refer to the final chapter eight—"Reminiscences of the Diner".

"Early years at Gilley's Wagon," author unknown:

Every evening, except Monday, at a little after five o'clock, Kennedy's Diner rolls into Portsmouth ready for business as usual and alights on the Square beside the North Church. The last of its kind in Portsmouth, this portable lunch cart is an anachronistic eye-stopper for newcomers, but has become a familiar sight to every native of Portsmouth.

Bill Kennedy has been in the lunch cart business since August 1918. Years ago, after the turn of the century, there were several diners-on-wheels in Portsmouth, but for the last 25 plus years there has been only one. Bill recalls that the first wagon he used was a small, light, horse-drawn affair, which had to sit on the Square through the winter because it couldn't be pulled through the snow.

During the Depression the diner used to give free supper to 15–20 people at night, even though its own bills were months in arrears. 'It was an awful struggle,' Bill says, 'but we made it.'

Besides the owner, the lunch cart is operated by a staff of two. Ralph Gilbert, better known as 'Gilley,' works alone serving customers and prefers it that way. He says that anyone else behind the counter would be a nuisance. Bill says that if Gilley quit tomorrow, he would, too.

In the daytime the diner sits over on Court Street, where every afternoon, Warren Kohl, the set-up man, makes the coffee, fills the food and drink reefers, and takes care of general cleaning and maintenance.

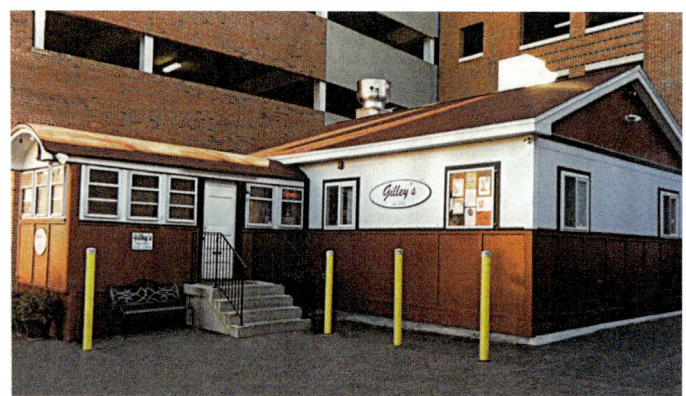

Gilley's PM Lunch (diner) was once known as the White House Café when it traveled through the streets of Fall River, MA. This diner was built in 1939 by the Worcester Diner Car Co. and was permanently placed on Fleet Street, Portsmouth, NH. *Photo courtesy of the author.*

Public Reviews of Gilley's PM Lunch Wagon:

November 1, 2009—There is no better late snack in Portsmouth. Don't even waste your time or money on another place for a quick after br stop.

Signed,
Customer,
Portsmouth, NH

May 2, 2010—If you think of Gilley's as a restaurant, you're going to be disappointed. It's a tiny trailer that has probably been there since the Civil War. It's open until 2am (I think) and it's the place to go for dogs, burgers, and fries after an evening of entertainment or for a quick lunch. Go, have a burger and some cheese fries, and experience a bit of what Portsmouth, NH is all about. And if there's no place for you to sit inside and you have to leave, that's how it goes.

Signed,
nhunixguy
New Hampshire

April 14, 2010—Great little spot that serves up the usual burgers and dogs. It's nothing flashy, just a simple place for afternoon/late night grub!

Signed,
troy mcclure
Boston, MA

Date unknown—Gilley's is an old-fashioned night-owl lunch wagon, now semi-permanently anchored on Fleet Street, where it used to arrive each night around supper time. According to legend, the proprietor received a ticket every evening, but business was so good that he considered the fine simply a cost of doing business and kept coming back. Today, Gilley's has an address and even a telephone number; and while it is not, as far as we know, a scofflaw anymore, it has maintained a delicious ambience. It is in the wee hours of the morning, and all the normal restaurants are closed and even the bars are shut, you can count on Gilley's to be serving up hamburgers with chocolate milk on the side to a rogue's gallery of city folk who range from derelicts to debutantes.

Men dine while standing on the sidewalk, but there is some limited indoor seating at a narrow counter opposite the order area and galley kitchen. Gathered here under some of the most unflattering lighting on earth are insomniacs, die-hard parties, and late-shift workers with no other place to eat, feasting on such quick-kitchen fare as hot dogs with sauerkraut, French fries gobbed with cheese, and fried egg sandwiches with coffee on the side. The best in the house, or at least the one that seems most appropriate in the restaurant, is the hamburger, actually the cheeseburger…no, make that a double cheeseburger, with bacon and onions, too.

Signed,
Jane and Michael Stern

Heritage Diner claimed to be the oldest operating Worcester Diner in the country; however, the distinction really belongs to Casey's Diner in Natick, Massachusetts.

According to historian Randy Garbin, the following history is given:

In 1997, the efforts of the LaPierre family allowed this beautiful diner to reemerge after years of being hidden behind a clapboard façade and pitched roof. When known as Alice's Trolley Stop, the diner's exterior revealed little of its true origin, with the possible exception of the window proportions, although it interior still had many of the original features.

The diner came to Charlestown in 1946 and opened as the L & Y Diner, but in the early 1970s, its owner wrapped it in artificial siding. In 1997, Carol LaPierre and her husband came to the rescue. As the LaPierre's uncovered the diner, they also revealed one of the original wheels used to move it. Since then, they've successfully revived the diner and created a fine place to eat.

The diner had been well maintained and had retained much of the 1920s original heritage and friendly atmosphere, unfortunately, the diner is presently closed.

Hillsborough Diner, formerly known as Caron's Restaurant, is a rare 1940s classic Kullman in Hillsborough, New Hampshire. It is only one of two Kullman Diners in all of northern New England. The diner was moved to New Hampshire from New Jersey in the 1960s. Mary Caron runs this smoke-free diner and served all the traditional favorites in the 1940s which is the only one located in New Hampshire; American food is the specialty.

The diner is your typical town diner with a brick building addition. The front of the diner has a lunch counter, seating booths, and there is also a regular casual dining room to the left and a kitchen in the rear. The food is considered to be basic American generic fare.

The main menu offers fried appetizers, salad, soup, chili, comfort food, pasta dishes, seafood, sandwiches, wraps, grinders, diet plates, desserts featuring baklava, pies, puddings, ice cream, floats and frappes. Senior and kids' menu are also available.

The diner is located at 83 Henniker in Hillsborough, New Hampshire (Note: Take U.S. 202 traffic around the town of Hillsborough, as Miss Caron's Diner is near the heart of town.)

Public Reviews for Hillsborough Diner:

April 18, 2008—I had breakfast here recently. I sat myself at the lunch counter (stools) and the waitress offered fresh ground brewed coffee. I had the Breakfast Wrap with Egg Beaters, cheese & sausage served with pan fried. The wrap came out in 10 minutes and tasted decent. The pan fries were okay and potatoey. The coffee mug was big, so I only needed one refill on coffee. An overall decent breakfast with good service. I was golden and good to go!

Signed,
Customer

September 29, 2011—If you want fresh fish, I'd say this is the place to go in Hillsborough. Supposedly, the owner goes to Massachusetts himself every week to pick up fresh seafood. No frozen fish delivery truck here. The fried seafood platter is a small mountain of seafood, fried, and onion rings. And they don't load it up with fries and onion rings and scrimp on the fish. It is a very generous portion. Most everything else is homemade there and the food is pretty darn good for a little diner in a small town. Worth a slight detour off the 202/9 bypass.

Signed,
Customer.

Hope's Diner is a choice classic diner that relives the 50s in a perfect way. The diner is conveniently located on 127 Plaistow Road, Plaistow, NH 03865.

Public Reviews of Hope's Diner:

August 10, 2012—This is a great place for a classic diner experience. The menu is classic eggs and sandwiches. The last diner that went avant-garde at this location, Diner #317, went under rather quickly. Early Bird down the street has a wider menu, but feel more like a cafeteria in comparison. Also, Early Bird closes earlier. Since we are night owls, I appreciate that Hope's Diner is open until 2.

Signed,
Barbara B.
Winchester, MA

July 9, 2012—OK, this place has undergone many names changes so we were a little wary. Although it was not advertised on the menu, I ordered an egg white omelet loaded with veggies, hash browns and toast. They will accommodate almost any request even if not on the menu.

This was the best egg white omelet I've ever had in my life. There wasn't too much egg, not too much cheese, it was just right. I could taste every ingredient that went into it, and the veggies tasted as if they had just gone out back and picked them out of a garden. In other diners they load up on the cheese inside and then sprinkle more on the outside and it's just over kill. Here, they use just the right amount. PERFECT!

The hash browns were crispy but not greasy. The toast was perfectly buttered.

I did try some of my husband's meal. He had corned beef hash and home fries on his plate. Both were crispy but not greasy and both were delicious!! Perfectly cooked!

It's my favorite diner.

Signed,
Alysha C.
Plaistow, NH

Joey's Diner is a classic style diner, considered one of New Hampshire's fine diners, which is located at 1 Craftsman Lane, Amherst, NH 03031.

Public Reviews of Joey's Diner:

February 21, 2013—I have been to many diners in NY and NJ and I had such a good time at Joey's. It's just a simple, laid back diner with great 50s theme and wonderful atmosphere. I had no issue with the food because it was what it is DINER FOOD. The coffee was amazing. I drank four cups and didn't even realize it.

Siegfried is an amazing waiter. He's very family-oriented and fun to be around. If you're looking for a good start to a quiet Sunday, just enjoy a family meal at Joey's. Looking forward to going back during the summer!!

Signed,
Adrienne G.
West New York, NJ

February 19, 2011—Shiny aluminum on the outside of the building, shiny aluminum throughout the insides of the restaurant. Red vinyl seats, chromed-edged tables from the 1940's or 50's Coca Cola "door" serving as the entrance into the restrooms. Counter seating, bright lights and many tables and booths. Black and white checked flooring. Couches with front bumpers and replica airplanes and vintage cars hanging from the ceiling.

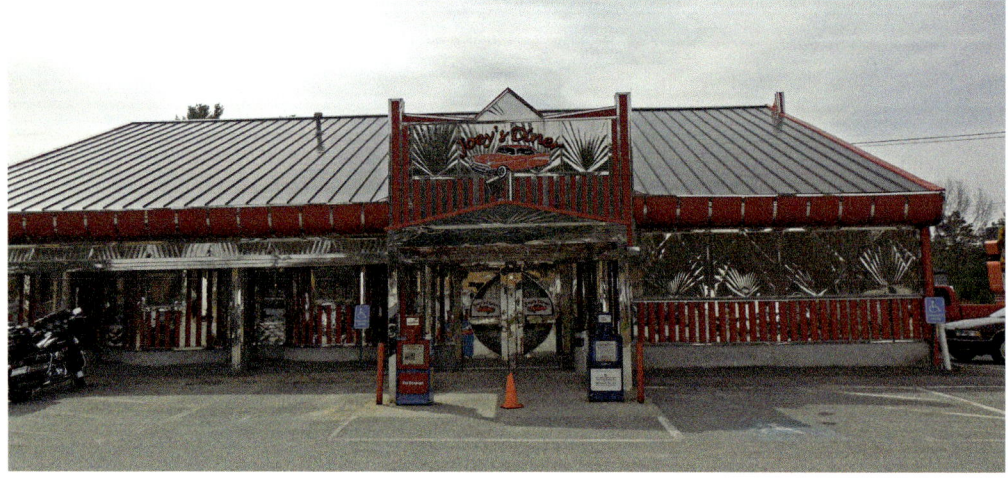

Exterior of Joey's Diner in Amherst, NH. *Photo courtesy of Ron Scully.*

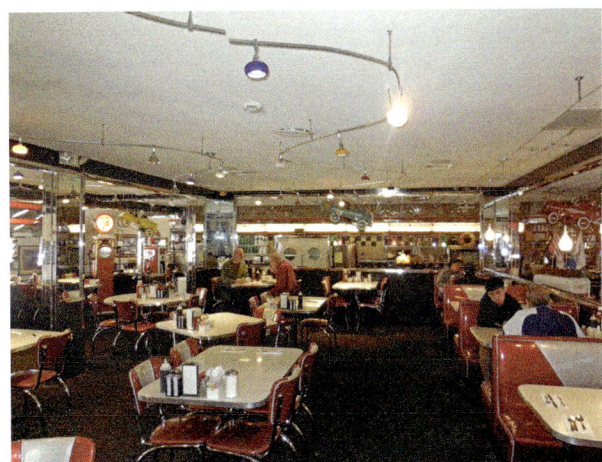

Glossy dining room of Joey's Diner in Amherst, NH. *Photo courtesy of Ron Scully.*

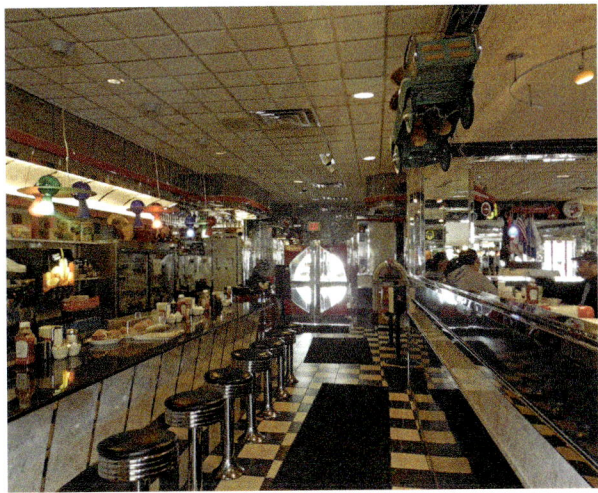

Lunch counter of Joey's Diner. *Photo courtesy of Ron Scully*

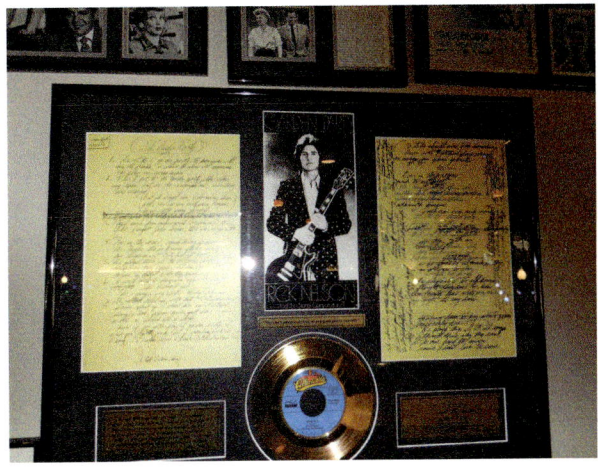

Ricky Nelson's 'Garden Party' in handwritten verse decorates the wall. *Photo courtesy of Ron Scully*

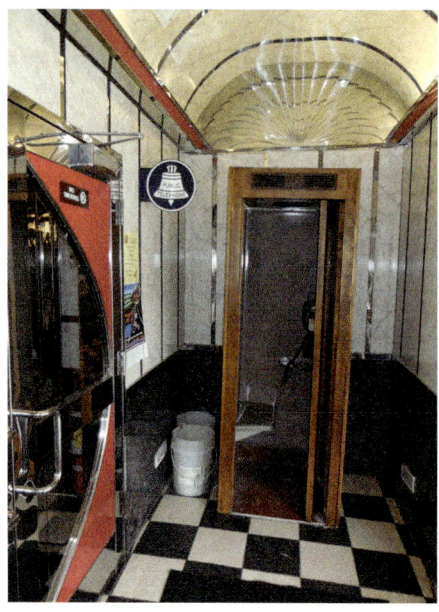

A Public telephone at Joey's. On this particular day plastic buckets rather spoilt the 'photographic ensemble'. *Photo courtesy of Ron Scully*

We don't usually have breakfast in a restaurant except if we're on vacation or when we want to get together with our family for a relaxing, casual meal. "Joey" is the husband of one of Mr. K's employees, who gave us a coupon, so off we went.

One can order breakfast all day, which is what we did at 11:30. We had coffee, 2 eggs with wheat toast and bacon, and crispy home fries, and a 3-egg omelet with cheese, peppers, and onions and wheat toast and home fried. And we shared 1 pancake with choc chips.

The place has sandwiches, club, wraps, salad, and entrees like steak tips and liver and onions, desert, a kid's menu, and senior menu, and of course, breakfast all day.

Signed,
Marcy K.
Chelmsford, MA

May 20, 2010—I love Joey's Diner! I think the food is absolutely excellent, love the atmosphere and do agree that the service is rather slow, but for me it's worth the wait. Their eggs benedict is AWESOME! I must admit that I like the fake hollandaise sauce. The powdered kind that comes out of an envelope that you mix with practically an entire stick of butter. The home fried are nice and crispy. They make excellent stuffed French toast which I'm assuming is stuffed with fruit/cream mixture. Joey offers you pick three combo which I love. Usually restaurants offer only 2 choices between soup, salad and sandwich, but at Joey's you can eat all three. The food is fairly cheap. Last time I went to Joey's, I ordered Poutine and it was absolutely delicious. Crispy French fries, smothered in beef gravy topped with melted cheese.
The service has been hit or miss, but for the most part everyone is very pleasant. I don't think it's fair to rate business on the fact that the waiter or waitress was slow, which has only happened to me on one occasion, so I'm giving Joey's 5 stars.

Signed,
Kristen F.
Hudson, NH

Lindy's Diner is the only 1960 Paramount diner in Northern New England. After nearly thirty years of ownership, this space-age styled diner was sold by the Rigopolous family. They served American food with Greek specialties.

In December 2003, the diner and property was sold again to Chuck Criss and Nancy Petreillo who were residents of Keene. After the purchase, both Chuck Criss and Nancy Petreillo continued the tradition of serving the public in the Greek diner tradition.

Lindy's Diner is located on 19 Gilbo Street, Keene, NH.

Public Reviews of Lindy's Diner:

April 13, 2013—We had heard so many good things about this diner, we had to stop on our way north. Typical diner, with typical food, but so cute!! They have the individual "Juke boxes" on the table/booths. Yes, it's dated, but it's a diner. Exactly what you'd expect. Our food was excellent, too much for us to eat...

Signed,
MarieinFitchburg
Fitchburg, MA

May 6, 2013—Stayed in Keene and stopped at Lindy's for breakfast. Waitress was very pleasant and efficient. Nicely cooked eggs, not overdone. In addition to regular bread they have a section of bread baked on the premises. I had the homemade multi-grain and it was very good. Menu

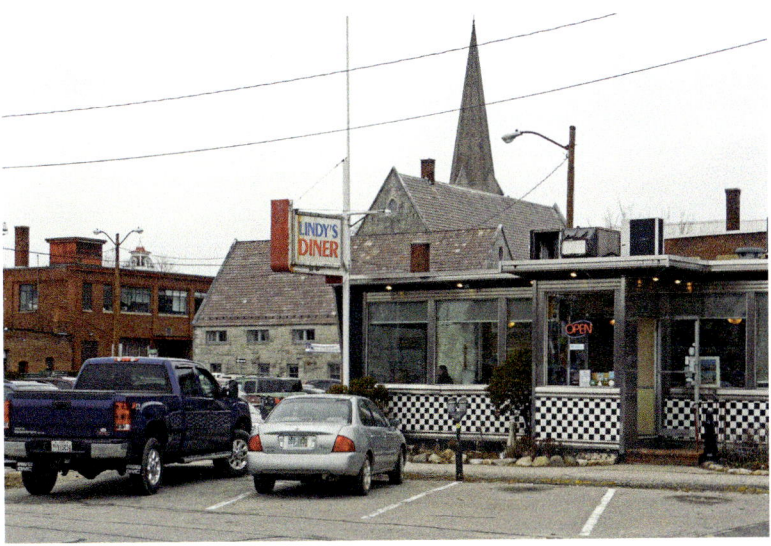

Exterior of Lindy's Diner in Keene, NH.
Photo courtesy of Ron Scully.

seemed to have one or two innovative twists on diner stables....

Signed,
Misplacedmidwest...
Baltimore, Maryland.

Littleton Diner, located in the Great North Woods, is thriving in the bustling town of Littleton, NH. It is one of the older diners in the state.

According to the advertisement the following is details are given:

The diner was built in Merrimack, Massachusetts in 1928 and was transported to Littleton where it opened for business in 1930. In 1940, thanks to Eugene and Stella Stone, a new Sterling Diner was built by J. D. Judkins on the same site where the old diner was originally located. The diner has served the community and travelers ever since. The diner was chosen Yankee Magazine Editor's choice in 2010 and the Food Network Magazine's 50 states. This is a must stop when traveling through the North Country. The diner is well known for serving classic diner food in an atmosphere of nostalgia of the glory days of the early diners.

The Stones kept the Littleton Diner until 1960 when they sold it to their daughter and her husband, Louis Burpee, and they operated it until 1975. During this time, the diner saw many owners.

It was Everett Chambers who stabilized the business and operation of the diner in 1992, but soon sold it in 2003 to Chris and Patti Williford. They continued to serve their clientele the classic diner good food and in the homemade style.

They serve a full American menu with daily specials and homemade desserts.

The diner is located at 170 Main Street, Littleton, NH 03561.

Public Reviews of Littleton Diner:

February 18, 2013—'Old School Diner'—You know the kind I am talking about. Pre-fab from the 1930's...plunked down right in the center of town, Good coffee, and decent, basic diner food at reasonable prices. I love these places for the atmosphere. If you are a fan of old school diners... this place is for you...

Signed,
Aussienels
Hartford, Connecticut

April 10, 2013—We love this place!! Great parking in the back and the food was delicious! We ate at the diner three times during our visit this weekend as it was also cost efficient. Definitely try the pancakes as they use flour made at the local gristmill! The waitress we had all three times was wonderful and social...

Signed, customer

May 29, 2013—My parents love this place. They often come Friday mornings early to get the Hobo Hash. I must admit that I like that breakfast, but the coffee is a let-down. I've been other days for breakfast and even for dinner and it has always been an 'ok' experience. They will continue to get my business.

Signed,
Imari 535

The Main Street Station diner is a Worcester Streamliner diner (#793), 1946. According to the catalogue it was formerly named Fracher's Diner until 2001; however, the name is still visible on the front façade. Several years ago, the diner was encased in brick, but that was removed. Originally, the diner was a converted train car with five small booths and 12-15 counter stools. The décor of the eatery is mainly old-time signs, keeping that old fashioned atmosphere with the dark wood of the window trim and wall which lends a cozy atmosphere.

The Main Street Station is located on 103 Main Street directly across from the Plymouth State University in Plymouth, NH 03264.

Public Reviews of The Main Street Station:

March 30, 2008—On our way to Waterville Valley, we stopped at the Main Street Station for breakfast located across the street from PSU. Formerly Fracher's Diner, the Main Street Station was voted New Hampshire's No. 1 Diner in Yankee magazine. This diner is open for breakfast and lunch only.

The front section of the diner (Worcester Streamliner #793 from 1946) has the old fashioned diner look with lunch counter stool seating and booths along the front windows. The lunch counter area is decorated with classic old train pictures. The attached back section houses the kitchen, restrooms, and another dining room with a small bar.

The breakfast menu offers egg dishes, omelets, eggs benedict, (6 kinds) quiche, pancakes, waffles, French toast, home fries & more. Additionally, Egg Beaters are 50 cents per egg and egg whites and centers 80 per egg. The lunch menu offers American and Tex Mex items including appetizers, burgers, sandwiches, wraps, salads, quiche, soup, chowder, chili, and desserts. Beer and wine available. There's a sign warning people in a rush that the food is not fast food since all of the food is prepared to order.

Signed,
Ian W.
Pelham, NH

April 26, 2009—Nestled in downtown Plymouth across from Plymouth State University, Main Street Station (formerly Fracher's Diner) is a quaint spot for a healthy breakfast or lunch. A converted rain car, the diner has about 5 small booths and 12–15 counter seats. Décor is mainly old-time signs, keeping that old-fashioned feel, and the dark wood of the window trim and wall lends a cozy atmosphere. Service is pleasant and not rushed. The portions are generous and the prices reasonable.

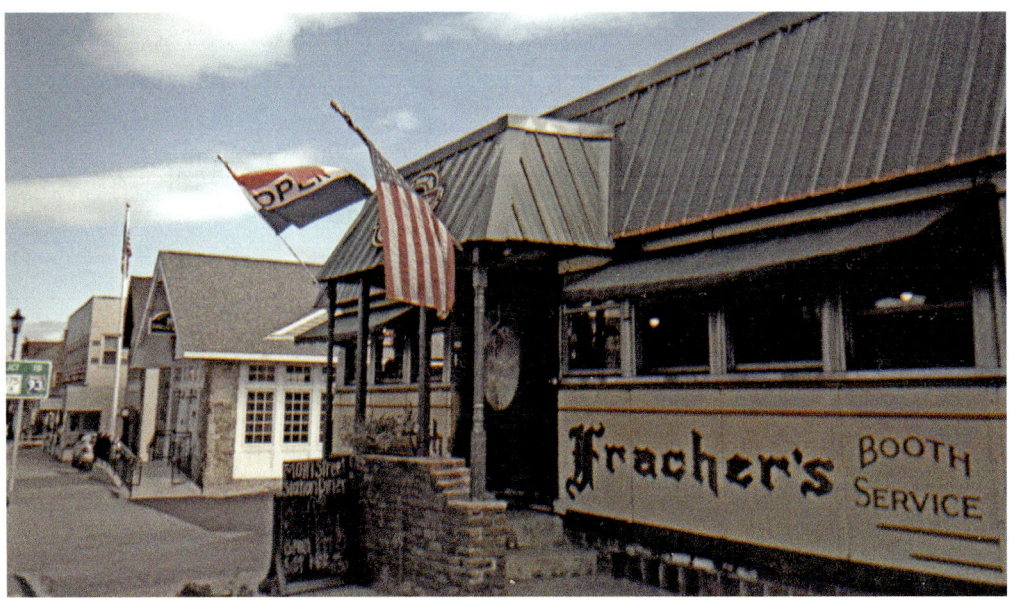

Main Street Station (Diner) is a Worcester Streamliner (#793) built in 1946. It is presently located on Main Street in Plymouth, NH. *Courtesy of the author.*

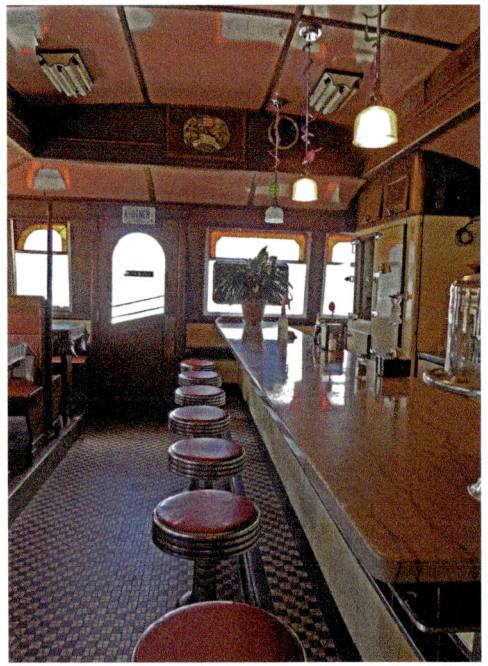
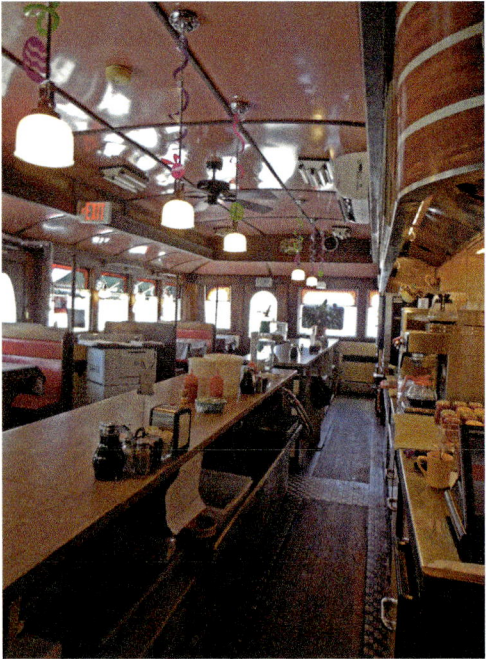

Left: The counter inside of Main Street Station. *Photo courtesy of Ron Scully.*
Right: A view of the booths, from behind the counter. *Photo courtesy of Ron Scully.*

My husband had the Breakman, which was poached eggs over pastrami and red peppers, served with home fries and toast. I had the pancake Hole-In-One, which was 3 eggs over easy on top of two thick and fluffy pancakes, served with home fries and sausage. Everything was great. I like how they make the home fries with sautéed peppers and onions—yum! Pancakes were thicker that how most places make them, and very tasty. We had a satisfying filling breakfast for less than $20.

Signed,
Liz P.
Shirley, MA.

On January 22, 2011—We found this great little place on our way back from Loon with a search on Google (thanks Google). We stopped there for breakfast and were happily surprised by the funky character. Its front entrance area is a real Worcester Diner. Very cool. We were seated promptly in a back dining area and immediately served coffee, which was nice cause it was a frigid day. Now for food. I had Breakman, which is two perfectly poached eggs over grilled pastrami and red peppers. I had never ever seen this on a menu before. It was beyond my expectations, and totally delicious. My wife had a dish named Iris Eggs Benedict that was a poached egg on corned beef hash and an English muffin with hollandaise sauce. Also, delicious. My brother in law had Denver omelet and he pretty much inhaled it. My sister in law had a vegetarian omelet called the Californian that she said was awesome. The service was very attentive but not overdone. The menu is very eclectic. We went a little bit off the path to go to the Main Street Station and feel lucky that we did.

Signed,
Dave B.
Boston, Massachusetts

Mary Ann's Diner opened for business in 1989:

> ...with the idea of giving to our customers the best service, homemade food, and atmosphere we could. Without any previous restaurant experience we waited on our customers the way we would like to be waited on when we go out to eat. The servings are the size we would like to have when we dine out in an atmosphere we would love to dine in.
>
> We have gained so many friendships out of our awesome clientele and would like to thank each and every one of you for your continued patronage. Thank you. The Andreoli Family and staff at Mary Ann's.

The diner is conveniently located on 29 E Broadway, Derry, NH 03038.
Public Reviews of Mary Ann's Diner:

March 24, 2010—The absolute BEST breakfast in the area. The food is delicious and not too pricey. I love the Irish Eggs. The wait staff is always friendly, I love my coffee and they never leave me with an empty cup!

The decor is fantastic. The vibe really just livens you up. I could spit out all the wonderful qualities I could think of, but the fact of the matters is, you have NO IDEA until you go!! There is a reason people wait in line Saturday and Sunday morning to eat here!!

Signed,
Katelyn W.
Plaistow, NH

October 17, 2010—I grew up in Derry and if it weren't for my parents still being there, I wouldn't have much reason to visit it again. One draw that's still difficult to resist—breakfast at MaryAnn's. I once met John Kerry here while he was running for President. Derry is short enough on Democrats that you can get pretty close to them when they have appearances.

I'm picky about my breakfast and brunch fare—I just think many places do it poorly, and sad as it sounds, it's pretty easy to ruin eggs. Good home fries are hard to come by. And some places can't get French Toast right. Here you get all of the stables of a good breakfast, all done just right. Portions are solid—not skimpy but not contributing to the obesity epidemic either. And the servers—always friendly, dressed to match the 50's décor.

I just wish MaryAnn's was open a little later, because the urge to eat breakfast food can hit at any time.

Signed,
David V.
Arlington, VT

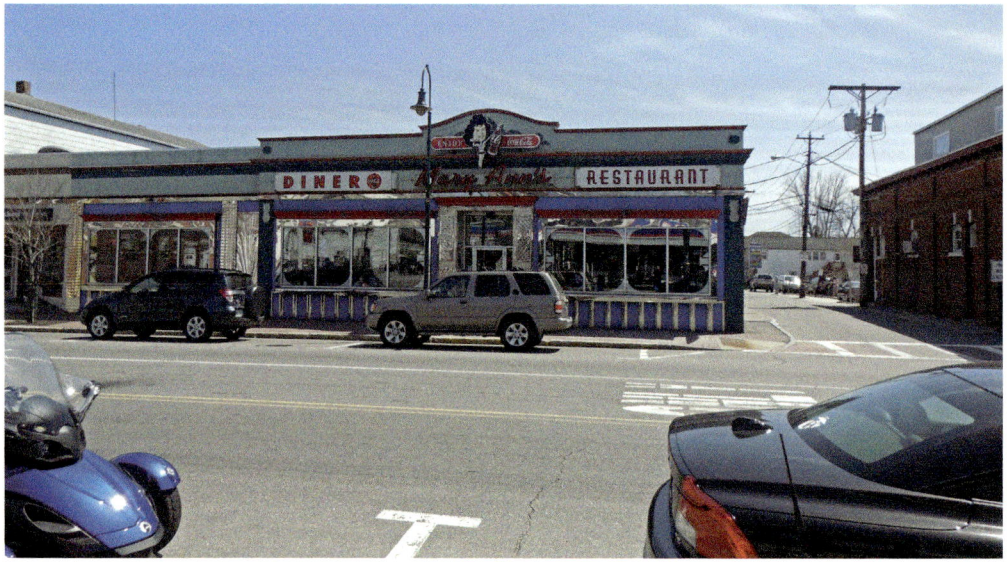

Mary Ann's Diner in Derry, NH. *Photo courtesy of Ron Scully.*

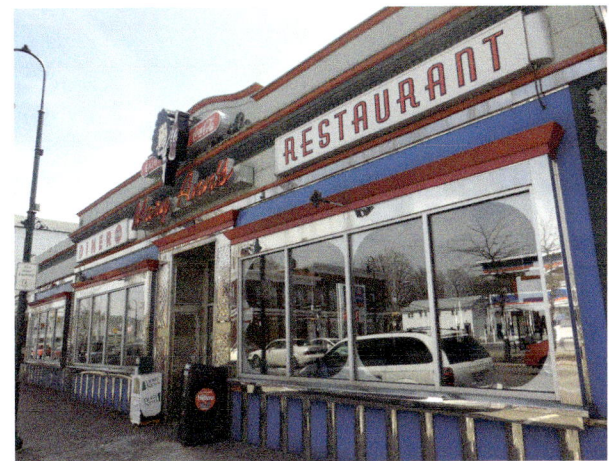

Exterior of Mary Ann's Diner in Derry, NH. *Photo courtesy of Ron Scully*

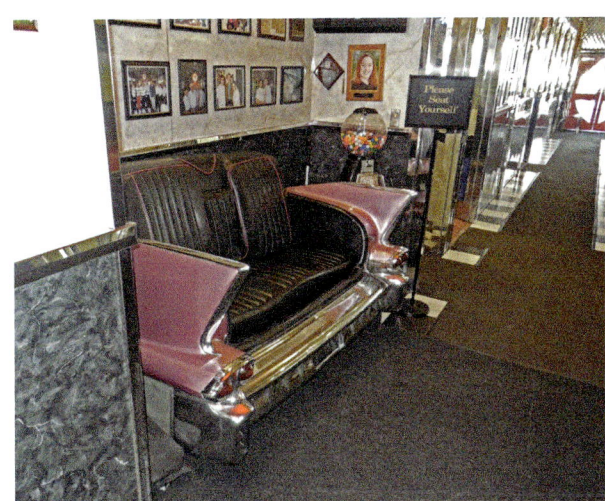

'For waiting only' at Mary Ann's. *Photo courtesy of Ron Scully*

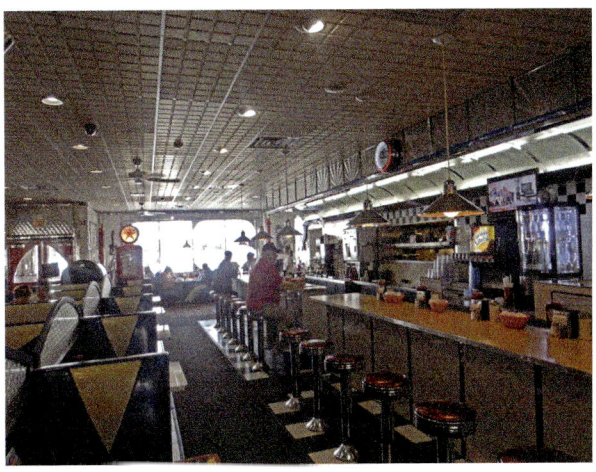

vColorful interior of the diner. *Photo courtesy of Ron Scully*

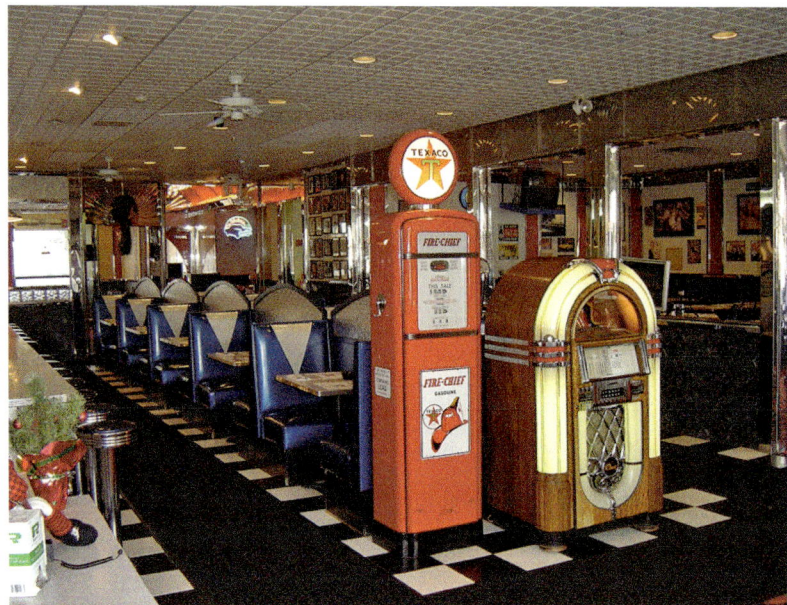

Period relics at Mary Ann's Diner in Derry, NH. *Photo courtesy of Ron Scully*

May 12, 2011—When it comes to breakfast food, it is pretty important in my book that I get quantity and quality. I had a breakfast that had a little bit of everything—pancakes, home fries, toast, eggs, and beans. Everything for under $5! Add in coffee and a side of bacon, and you are really living.

It was all very good. Fluffy pancakes and expertly cooked eggs and potatoes. When you are that packed late on a Saturday morning, you know the staples are going to be fresh and done right. To top it off, the portions were pretty big. Not unreasonably large, but bigger than most.

Service was friendly, with all of the cheesy 50s nostalgia sitting there on display. It is small town New Hampshire at its finest.

Stop by MaryAnn's for a hearty, fun, and delicious breakfast.

Signed,
Matt L.
Salem, NH.

The Meredith Diner was one of the finest vintage Worcester Diners in 1935. The diner operated through the mid-1960s. This celebrated diner was owned and operated by Carl and Marion Chase, and was a popular gathering place and social magnet for the townspeople of the community. It was not uncommon to find the diner filled beyond capacity after school basketball games, dances, concerts, plays, and Friday and Saturday night socials. They were best known for their fine food and hospitality. Note Carl Chase's new Cadillac at the side door.

The location of the diner was on Main Street, Meredith, NH—no longer there.

Miss Wakefield Diner is owned and operated by Scott Braham since 1998. The management of Miss Wakefield Diner has provided the following history of the diner:

> The diner is a 1949 O'Mahony diner. It was originally located in East Greenbush, NY where it was known as Pat and Bob's Diner. It opened there until 1968 and ended up in a junkyard. In 1991 the diner was found in storage near Albany, NY for quite some time, it had been vandalized and was in need of major restoration work. At that time the new owners had moved the diner to its present location. It was no easy task as she weighs nearly thirty tons, and is over sixteen feet wide. It was purchased, restored and moved to its present location. Many hours were taken to get her into the shape she is today, which is the shape she was when she was first built. This was his answer of many years of dreams.

Miss Wakefield Diner is located in Wakefield, NH, on Route 16; 7 Windy Hollow Rd., 03872.

Scott Braham presents the following:

> A diner is something everyone relates to. People of all socio-economic backgrounds come to eat at the diner. From the very wealthy to the guy with a roll of quarter—they all come and eat hearty meals and enjoy friendly conversations. I have great help. I hire good people and they tend to stay for quite a while. I don't believe in minimum wage, so I pay fairly well.
>
> Miss Wakefield Diner is one of only 22 operational diners manufactured under the name of Jerry Mahoney. Mahoney actually invented the diner. This particular unit originated in Albany, New York and went under the name of its owners—Pat and Bob. Pat and Bob's Diner was established in 1949 and operated until their retirement in 1968.

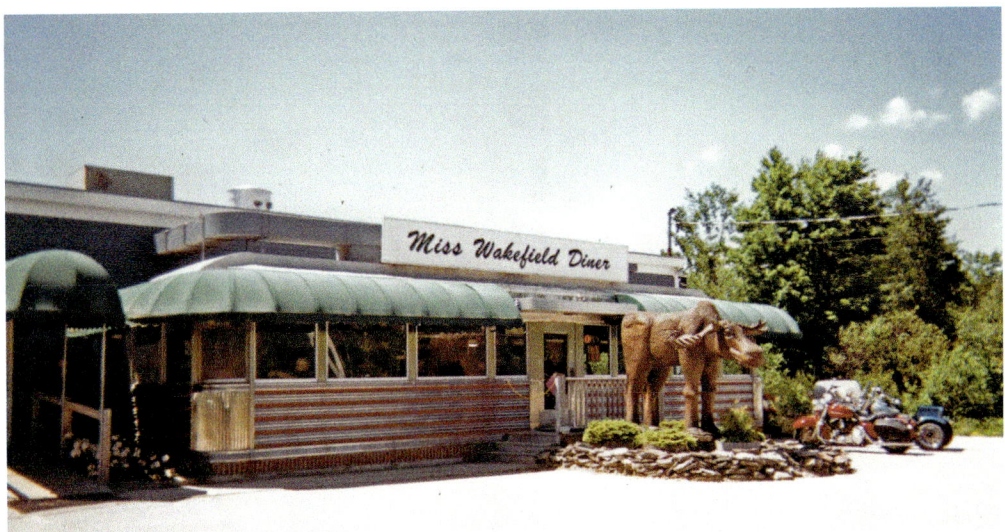

Miss Wakefield Diner is a O'Mahony Diner built in 1949. This classic diner is one of the few diners manufactured under the name of Jerry O'Mahony. *Photo courtesy the author.*

From its Route 16 location, passersby include lake-bound families in the summer, leaf peepers and hunters in the fall, and, of course, skiers all winter long.

Despite the arduous tasks involved in operating a diner, Bramer wears his happiness in his work. The diner is considered perfect breakfast and lunch stop.

Public Reviews of Miss Wakefield Diner:

February 14, 2010—I live in the area of the diner, my wife and myself frequent there at least 2 times if not more.

To the person that said they felt like they were being herded like cattle, what do you expect when you drove in and saw the parking lot full? And as far as those who didn't get their food the way they asked, those of us natives that live here year round don't like being talked down to. I have been there on occasion when several out-of-staters were very rude to the help. So if you're being a jerk about things the girls and the owner will fire rite back at you.

The food is outstanding. I always leave full and when it's time for the next meal I generally will pass as I'm stuffed from what I ate before. As far as the price, you get your money's worth and then some. It's an honor to have such a great eating establishment in the town I call home.

Signed,
Customer.

June 15, 2009—My husband and I stop here quite often when we are heading south. We think this is the best. The waitresses are very friendly and the service and the food is excellent. The owner is very friendly, and when he has a minute he comes out from the back and says a friendly 'hello, and how are you doing'. He remembers his costumers. Great place to eat!!!!!

Signed,
Maurice and Pat
customers

Mt. Pisgah Diner is a 1941 Worcester diner (#769). This quaint diner's façade was covered over and the interior has been painted, but retains a warm atmosphere. The food is a basic American menu—breakfast and lunch hours.

The diner is located at 118 Main Street, Winchester, NH 03470.

Public Reviews of Mt. Pisgah Diner:

April 5, 2010—The Mt. Pisgah Diner is an authentic Worcester Diner (*circa* 1930s), located along Main Street in Winchester. The atmosphere inside is very classic and cozy with stools seating at the long lunch counter with an open grill and 4 booths near the front windows.

The standard American diner food is offered for breakfast and lunch including eggs, pancakes, Texas French toast, omelets, hash, home fries, sandwiches, burgers, salad, soup and sides. New England Coffee is brewed here.

Specials are posted above the counter. The prices here are very reasonable.

The food was pretty basic, a folded soft scrambled egg, deep home fries (fresh cut potatoes), buttered white toast slightly over toasted, and ham. The coffee was just right, not too strong nor weak. There was just enough to get my day going.

Signed,
Ian W.
Pelham, NH

November 9, 2012—On the road early, looking for breakfast while avoiding "Fast Food." I was passing through Winchester and saw the non-descript diner. The inside of the diner is quite original with the counter seating and some window booths. I had a typical American breakfast, 2 eggs, bacon, home fries, toast and coffee. The service was great. Friendly conversations and very local customers, most folks were greeted by name.

Signed,
Mike W.
Warwick, RI

Olde Bay Diner is nestled on the shore of Alton Bay, Lake Winnipesaukee. It appears small but it is a very attractive and typical classic diner reminiscent of the '50s.
 The Olde Bay Diner is located in Rt. 11, Alton Bay, New Hampshire.

Public Reviews of Olde Bay Diner:

January 20, 2011—This place is A-OK. Since I was eating healthy, I was satisfied with my egg sandwich and fruit. I was lucky enough to try some food off the plates of those around me, and the homemade cinnamon swirl bread was amazing. The western omelet was huge and quite tasty too. Home fried looked awesome too!

Signed,
Pam O.
Lowell, MA

April 4, 2011—Went to this place first time ever though I grew up spending my summer's here. I am on a new health kick, and the Scrambled Eggs and Peppers we not greasy, or scary looking. Home fries were very light on the oil. Great prices and great service. If you are trying to be health conscious, stay away from the Sausage Patti's. While they were DELICIOUS, they tasted too good to be GOOD FOR ME as well.

Signed,
Sarah M.
Concord, NH

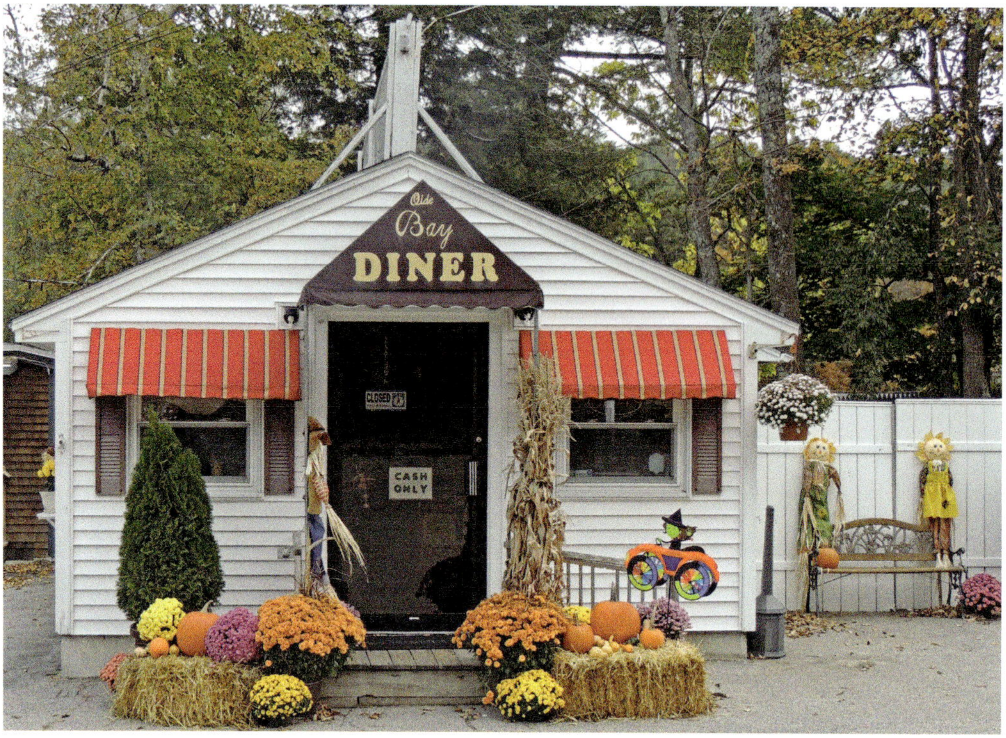

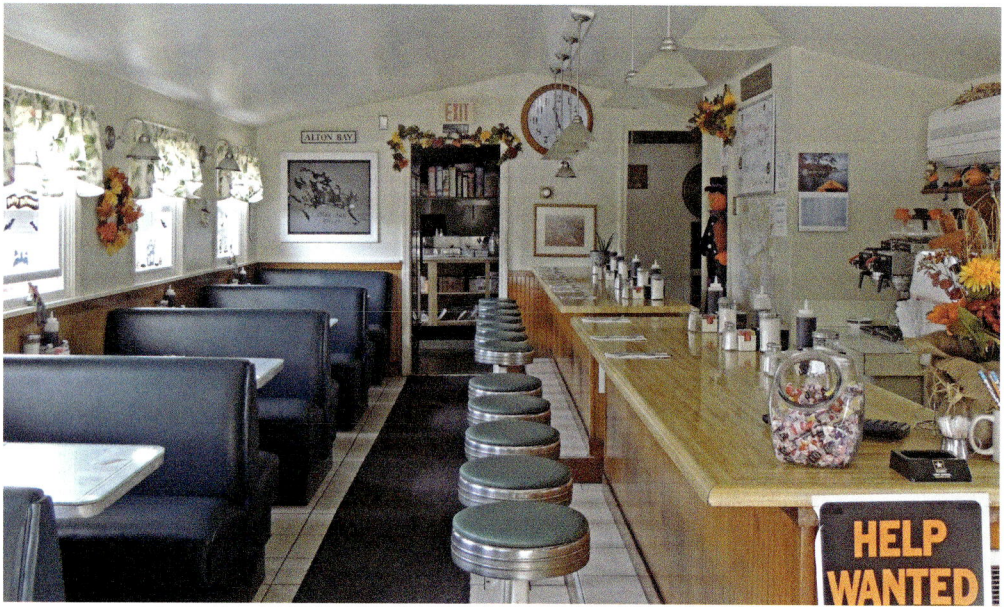

Olde Bay Diner is one of the few classic diners of the '50s, and its home is at the most southerly tip of Lake Winnipesaukee in Alton Bay, NH. *Photo courtesy of the Olde Bay Diner*

A clean well-lighted place. *Photo courtesy of Olde Bay Diner*

Peterborough Diner is a perfect example of a 1950s Worcester diner (#827). This classic diner was placed in Peterborough in 1949. An interesting history has been provided by the owners of the diner follows:

> If you visit the Peterborough Diner and sit on the left side counter from the entrance, you will see a food window where the kitchen sells the food. Under the window is a shelf. That shelf is actually a door that is flipped over. This location was where the food used to be prepared on a grill. That grill has been removed and innovative reconstruction placed it in a larger area in back.
>
> For the 1st year anniversary of new ownership, the staff and owner invited the community to a Classic car Cruise and Cook Out. We believe the best way to celebrate is to invite the community. Face painting, a live DJ playing oldies music, kid's games, and giveaways were among the festivities.

The Peterborough Diner is located at 10 Depot Square, Peterborough, NH 03458.

An interesting timeline of the diner is posted at the Peterborough Library as follows:

> Before 1936—Frank and Dora Ryan had a wooden diner on Grove Street. They purchased a used diner and placed it on the Depot Square site after the flood of 1936. In 1946 Milton Fontaine purchased the old diner. (The land belonged to the Boston & Maine Railroad)
>
> In 1950 the Worcester Dining Car Company built a new diner. It was the first one made in dark green and cream. This diner was placed on the same site as the old one.
>
> In 1955 Milton Fontaine sold the diner to his brother Edward Fontaine.
>
> In 1983 Edward Fontaine retired, selling the diner to Douglas Bartlett and Don Merwin.
>
> In 1984 Theofanis & Jane Athansopolos and Andy & Stacey Pirovolisanos bought the diner. The grand opening of the diner was on April 23, 1984.
>
> In August 2003 New owners, Patrick Healey and Eric Finley bought the diner. They are natives of New Hampshire.

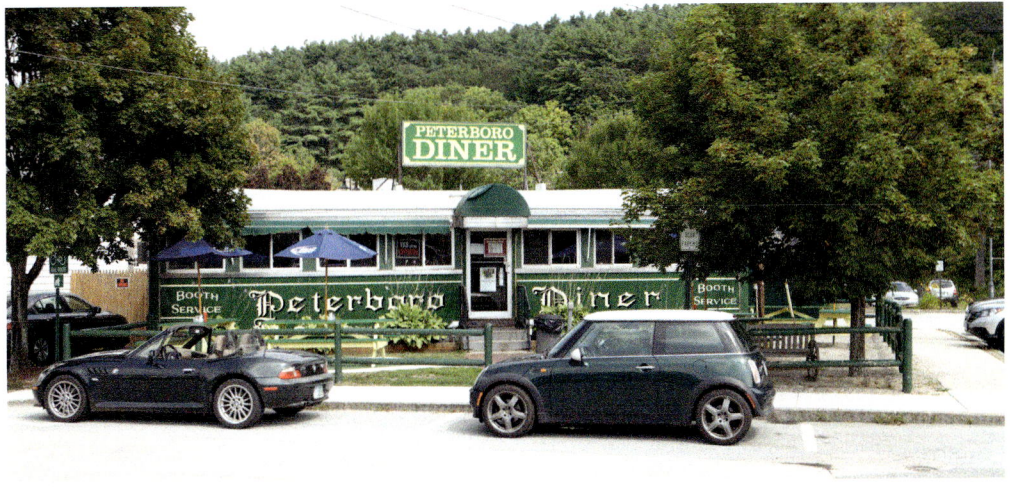

The Peterboro Diner is a Worcester Diner (#827) and is located Depot Square, Peterborough, NH. *Photo courtesy Wayne Brink.*

In July 2004 a new menu for breakfast, lunch/dinner focused on quality food at great prices.

In August 2004 A Classic Car Cruise and cook-out celebrated the one year anniversary of the new owners.

In May 2008, Patrick Healey became the sole owner of the Peterborough Diner.

Plain Jane's Diner is an example of the classic 1954 O'Mahony stainless design diner; it was manufactured in Elizabeth, NJ. According to the owners the following history is given:

> It started in business as Bells Pond Diner in Hamphariesville, NY, and was later relocated to Rumney, New Hampshire in 1990 by Bob and Gloria Merrill. The current owners, Jeff and Vicki Day purchased the diner in 2004. The diner is virtually unchanged from the original. Full menu of American food.

Plain Jane's has become a destination for the tourist and local guests in the White Mountains and Lakes Region areas.

The diner is located just before the Polar Caves at 897 Rte. 25, Rumney, NH 03266.

Public Reviews of Plain Jane's Diner:

> September 24, 2012—The service is good, breakfast plentiful and the dinners are truly home style comfort food. At dinner we have tried the Meatloaf and Shepherd's Pie, both very good. The Coconut Cream Pie is worth the trip! We love the oldies they play!

Signed,
Marjorie C
Wentworth, NH

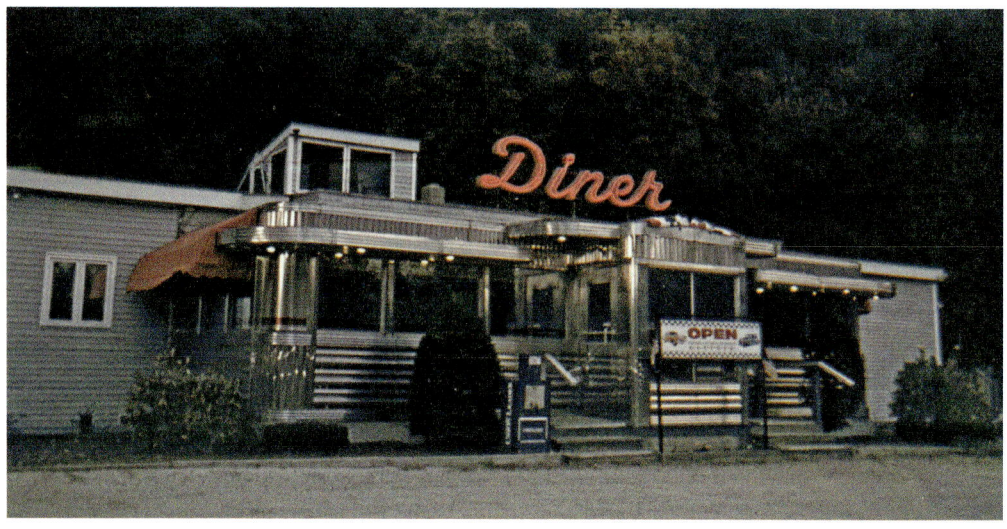

Plain Jane's Diner is an O'Mahony Diner from 1954. The diner was originally known as Bell's Pond Diner in New York. The diner was moved to its present location in Rumney, NH, in 1990. *Photo courtesy the author.*

November 3, 2012—Had a great home style lunch here as we were driving from Vermont through New Hampshire. It's old, of course, but I found it to be clean and well-kept too - stayed true to nostalgic style of the old airstream diner. Service was great and helpings were big. I loved the 50's feel and we both loved our food. ...

Signed,
Cindy 12
Orlando, FL

May 4, 2013—We always stop here when passing through. Some days we have a big breakfast there and I order a sandwich to take for lunch. A lot of choices on the menu, the food is always good and the portions are big and it is always clean.

Signed,
Cindy P
NH

Red Arrow Diner is one of the more famous diners in New Hampshire. According to the management of the Red Arrow Franchise the following history is given:

The original founder was David Lamontagne. At one point in time, there were a total of five Red Arrow locations throughout the city. The name Levi Letendre also goes hand in hand with the Red Arrow. Levi worked for the Red Arrow for many years, then eventually bought it from the Lamontagnes, and ran it successfully until his retirement in 1978. His legacy continues to carry on at the Red Arrow. After a few more owners, and then finally in early 1987, the Red Arrow Diner was for sale and vacant for the first time since 1922. That is when Carol Sheehan purchased it and brought the diner back to life.

The local diner is often the focal point of the community, and the Red Arrow is certainly no different. We have always been on the cutting edge in the diner area. In May '98, we made the decision to go 'smoke-free.' This was absolutely unheard of in the diner business, but we did our research. Although it was a little nerve racking, especially when we were picketed in the week before we went smoke-free! Well, things just rocketed from there, then in September of that same year, we were 'Voted one of the top ten diners in the country' by USA Today. To this day people travel from all over the world to visit us. Ask to see our guest book and check it out for yourself. Then in 2000 the Red Arrow Diner was finally named a Manchester, NH City Landmark!

Mention politics and you will see anyone and everyone at the Red Arrow! This past primary was no different. We were followed by WashingtonPost.com and wow what a hoopla it was! 95% of the candidates visited the diner—some of them even twice—they like the food so much. We even saw the likes of Diane Sawyer, who walked in the front door and immediately scoped out our Dinah Fingers!

The Red Arrow has undergone many transformations since the early days, but one thing will never change and that is keeping up the quality and consistency that The Lamontagne's began back in 1922.

We continue to strive each and every day to provide you with the very best the Red Arrow 24 Hr. Diner has to offer!

By striving to stick to the simple formula of good food, low prices, courteous service, and a clean atmosphere, the diner has become a most desirable eating establishment. Randy Garbin of *Roadside Magazine* recommends the breakfast chili omelet. Let us not forget the pies—the brownie cream pie and soul-satisfying coconut cream. Don't forget the Blue Plate special—the food is served on blue plates.

The Red Arrow Diner is located on 61 Lowell Street, Manchester, NH 03101 and the Red Arrow Diner on 63 Union Square, Milford, NH, 03055.

According to the State paper, The *Union Leader*, the following review of the Red Arrow Diner was printed on 09-20-1998: "Manchester, regularly ranked among this country's top ten cities, now hosts a diner with the same bragging rights."

USA Today, the nation's largest circulation newspaper, placed the Red Arrow on Lowell Street among the nation's top 10 diners in a September 18 article:

The Red Arrow in Manchester placed along-side Los Angeles, Philadelphia, Jersey City and Providence. 'By sticking to the simple formula of good food, low prices, courteous service, and clean atmosphere, the Red Arrow packs 'em in.' wrote Randy Garbin, who also publishes *Roadside Magazine* . The ranking has meant a boom in business, said owner Carol Lawrence. And that comes on top of an 8 percent bounce in sales that [the management] attributes to going smokeless earlier this year. Nowadays, the lunch time line snakes out the door. 'It's just amazing,' Lawrence said. 'I didn't realize the notoriety would be this big.'

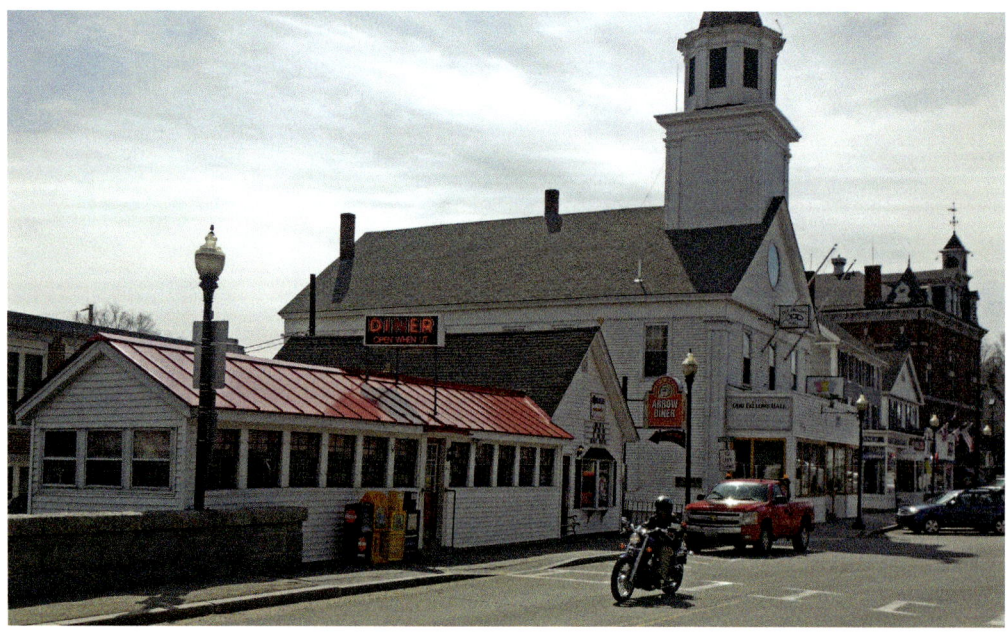

Red Arrow Diner opened their second diner in Milford, NH,t in October 2008. Since that opening, the Red Arrow Diner has been extremely successful. *Courtesy of Carol Lawrence and the Red Arrow Diner.*

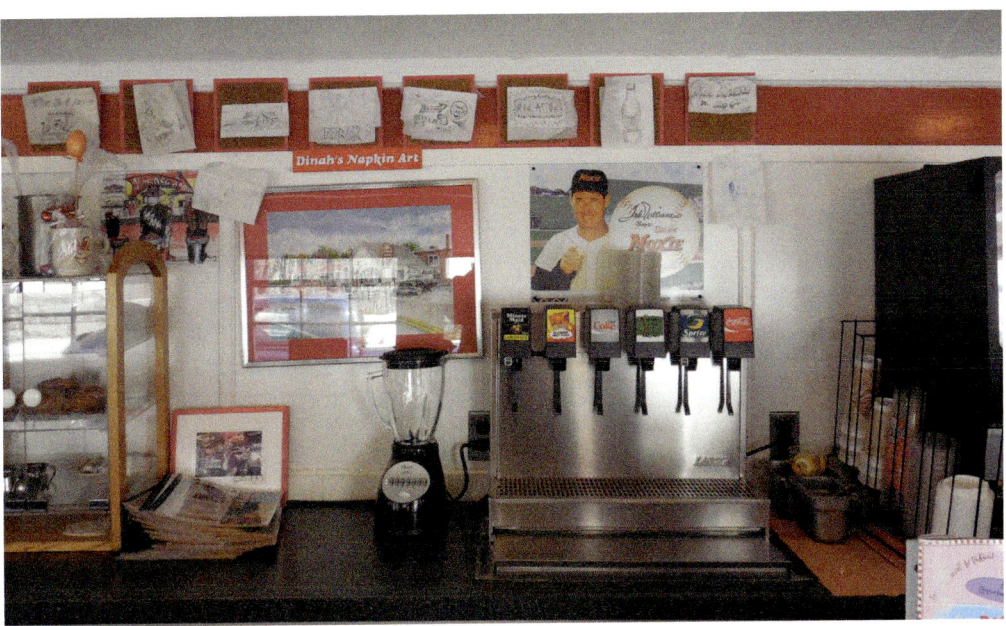

The Milford Red Arrow. *Photo courtesy of Ron Scully*

Customers have shown up from Baltimore, Oklahoma, Ohio and Scotland. One Chicago man read the article while flying in to Manchester, rented a car and drove up for a meal.

According to the *Roadside Magazine*, the following review of the Red Arrow Diner was printed on 07-18-1998:

Quickly becoming one of our favorite places, the Red Arrow Diner scored yet another direct hit with the public of Manchester, New Hampshire this weekend. On Saturday beginning at 11 AM, WQLL-FM 95.6 broadcast live in front of the diner, playing oldies and attracting customers new and regular to the downtown hotspot. And after this weekend, diner is the only meal we have to sample (and perhaps a lite night stop). During the visit, we enjoyed a good hearty breakfast which included the diner's chili omelet, and unusual concoction, but grilled without a hint of browning. Whoever Carol has working the grill obviously known his trade. Also, the coffee in this place is among the best we've tried. We hung around long enough to justify a piece of pie, and we tried the diner's own splendid brownie cream pie and the soul-satisfying coconut cream pie.

One final public review given by Jo Matyas as a special article for *The Star* was printed on 09-13-2007. (Jo Matyas is a freelance writer based in Kingston, Ontario, Canada. Her trip was subsidized by New Hampshire Tourism.):

MANCHESTER, N.H. By 8 a.m. it's possible 'even likely' that you'll have to wait for a seat at the Red Arrow Diner, a classic of its kind awash with scrubbed linoleum counters, neon signs and those clammy plastic chairs that stick to your skin.

You can tell the regulars and there are a lot of them by the slightly miffed looks on their faces. The Red Arrow has been running 24 hours a day since the doors opened in 1922, and the regulars like to know their stool at the long counter or their usual table hasn't been taken over by gawkers from out-of-town.

Daytime is easier than night. Try to snag a spot on any Saturday at 1:30 a.m. and you'll almost certainly have to stand in line.

'Our busiest shift is always the bar rush, 12:30 to 3:30 in the morning,' explains Carol Sheehan who became the third owner of the Red Arrow when she bought the business in 1987. Breakfast is popular all day.

About 5,400 eggs are served each week, about one every two minutes.

Things weren't always so good for the classic American roadside diner, In the 1950s, they were at the heart of a community. Romances blazed and fizzled in the booths. Business deals were sketched out on paper napkins; local gossip competed with whatever was hot on the jukebox. But roadside diners were edged out of the market by the rise of the ubiquitous fast-food joint, and by the late 1960s, business was in a serious slide.

Now, fueled by a nationwide wave clamoring for all that is nostalgic, the classic diner is enjoying a comeback, renovating, rebuilt and restored. And, once voted one of the top 10 diners in the country by USA Today, the Red Arrow seems to be leading the way.

Hometown boy Adam Sandler eats here when he's in town (there's a burger named after him). And the stools at the long counter have supported other public figures, like one-time vice-president Al Gore and Hollywood legend Paul Newman.

My waitress recommends anything with chili or the pie, even though the morning clock is still in single digits. The Red Arrow is famous for its chili (the breakfast menu has a highlighted box drawn around the famous hash brown special with grilled onions, chili and cheese $6.50 U.S.), its made-from-scratch pies (by the slice or whole pies to go), and of course that anytime breakfast menu that features different combinations of toast, eggs, bacon and sausages.

At one time, the City of Manchester was an industrial force to be reckoned with. Known as New Hampshire's 'Queen City,' an enormous complex of cotton spinning mills, stretching for two kilometers along the Merrimack River, was the economic engine that made the city the largest producer of cotton textiles in the world.

Along came the 1929 stock market crash, ushering in the Great Depression, Industrial cities around the world saw their power and strength come to a sudden end.

Along the wide, turbulent Merrimack River, a large-scale restoration of the decaying Amoskeag Mill yard began about 15 years ago, and in 2006 the classic red brick complex now home to offices, day spas, antique shops and upscale office space won a prestigious National Preservation Honor Award.

At the time of the 1929 stock market crash, The Red Arrow had only been open seven years. Barely enough time to set and records for customers served or eggs fried.

Years ago, there were five Red Arrow Diners in Manchester, but the original on Lowell St. is the only one that remains, the only one to weather the region's economic ups and downs. And it's the only one to see 'smoke free' dining becoming the norm.

'I still can't really believe it myself,' say Sheehan. 'It smells so nice in here now you can actually smell the food! The regulars seem to appreciate the change and business increased 20 per cent.

'People come in just to be entertained,' add my waitress. And that is a feeling even money can't buy.

Roundabout Diner is situated in the perfect location at the roundabout in Portsmouth, NH. At this busy intersection, the guest enters the front door and is immediately welcomed into this chic and most fashionable diner. This stylish, fashionable and marketable diner is a "concept" of a first-class restaurant. You might say that it would be considered a luxury grill, built to order by an old-line diner manufacturer. The food is good, and the service and hospitality is warm and welcoming.

According to the advertisement—"You can enjoy all your favorite diner classics. Excellent meals include burgers and sandwiches, Phantom Gourmet award-winning barbecue, comfort food classic like meatloaf, roast turkey, and the New England favorite fish and chips."

The diner is located at 580 US 1 (Portsmouth Traffic Circle), Portsmouth, NH 03801.

Route 104 Diner (Bobby's Girl)—This roadside diner has tastefully styled it to the 1950s when Elvis was king of Rock 'N' Roll.

If you enjoy good food, service and a '50s atmosphere, you will enjoy your eating experience at the Route 104 Diner. This diner was the last diner made by the Worcester Lunch Car Company in 1957, Worcester diner (#850). Its original operating location was on Rte. 6 in Johnston, Rhode Island. At the time it was known as Lloyd's Diner and had been located there until 1988.

Later, it was located in South Weymouth, Massachusetts, where it was attached to a nightclub called the Sh-Booms. Not many years later it was closed. The diner was then sold to John Keith who was brokering diners. Several buyers looked at the property until Alexis Stewart bought the diner with the intensions of operating it in Bridgehampton, Long Island, as The Delish Diner. After moving it to Long Island, the diner remained there in an empty field for two years.

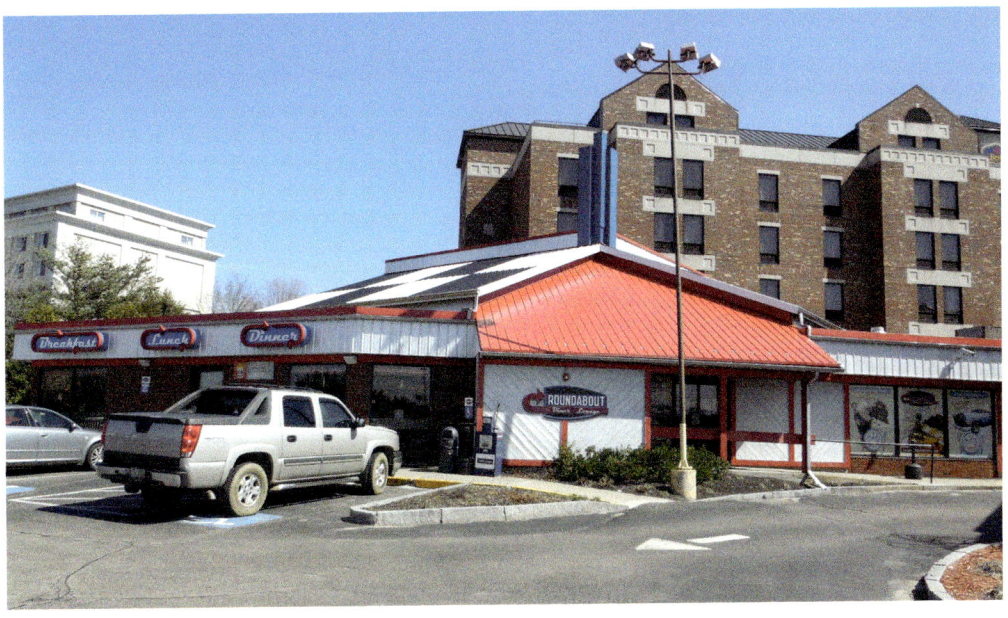

The Roundabout Diner in Portsmouth, NH. *Photo courtesy of Ron Scully*

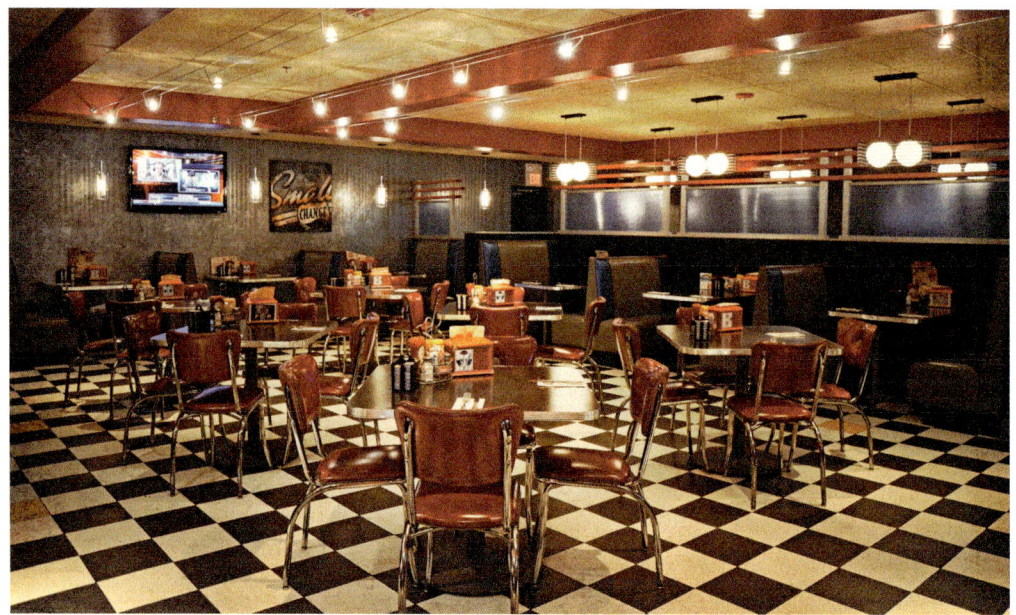

The interior banquet and special events room at the Roundabout Diner. *Photo courtesy of Ron Scully*

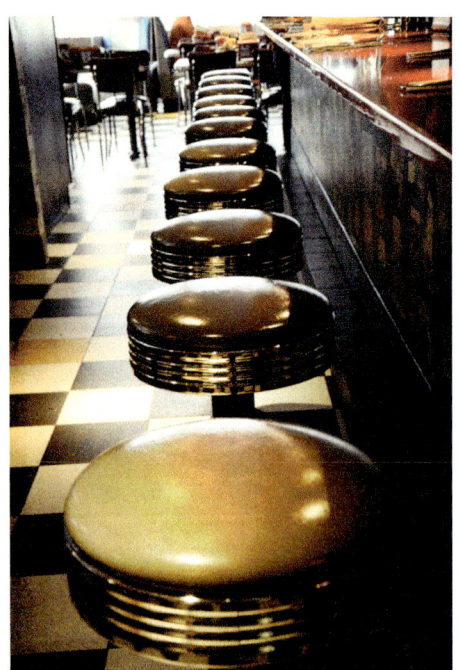
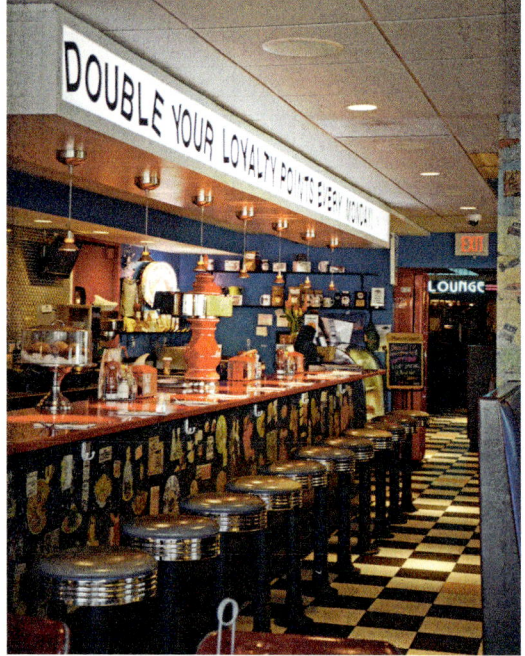

Left: The 'no waiting' lunch counter at the Roundabout Diner. *Photo courtesy of Ron Scully*
Right: A room colorful enough for kids. *Photo courtesy of Ron Scully*

It was Bob & Gloria Merrill who bought the diner in 1994, and had it moved to New Hampton, New Hampshire, and operated the diner under the name of Bobby's Girl Diner.

After three years of operation, the Merrill's sold the diner to Charlotte and Ed Kimball. The Kimball's owned and operated the diner for five years and finally closed the diner. A few years passed and the diner was purchased by Jane and Steve Green who spruced up the diner and gave it new life.

After many years of moving the diner from one location to another, this time the diner settled in New Hampton, New Hampshire, on Rt. 104. A main dining room was built on the rear of the diner so as to seat more guests and a collection of the Fifties memorabilia.

In 2002, Bob suffered a fall from a rooftop, and the Merrill's were forced to sell the diner. They sold it to Ron and Mary Elliard.

A few years ago, the Common Man Restaurant Corporation purchased Bobby's Girl and renamed it to become the Route 104 Diner. The Common Man family of restaurants presently owns and operates three great dinners: the Route 104 Diner, Tilt'n Diner, and The Airport Diner in Manchester.

This diner has a full menu of American food.

The Route 104 Diner is located in the Lakes Region on Route 104 just a few miles east on Interstate I-93, exit 23, New Hampton, NH 03862.

Public Reviews of the Route 104 Diner:

February 23, 2009—This diner is an institution. If you are driving along Rte. 104 from I-93 towards Meredith, then it is hard not to stop at this most attractive but typical looking like the diners of the '50s. It kind of calls out to you and is impossible to resist.

Try some home cooking in the famous 1950s-style roadside diner atmosphere. The tuna melt, barbeque pulled pork sandwich is a special luncheon, and for dinner try the homemade mac 'n cheese or shepherd's pie.

My Dad and I were once on a mission to find the best diner meal around, and we found it. Stop it and say hello.

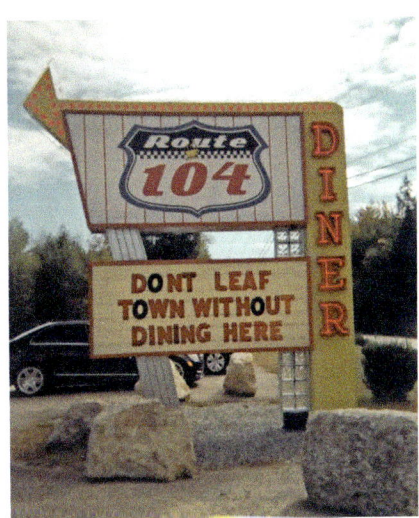

"Route 104 Diner sign on Route 104 in New Hampton directs travelling guests to the diner. *Photo courtesy of the author.*

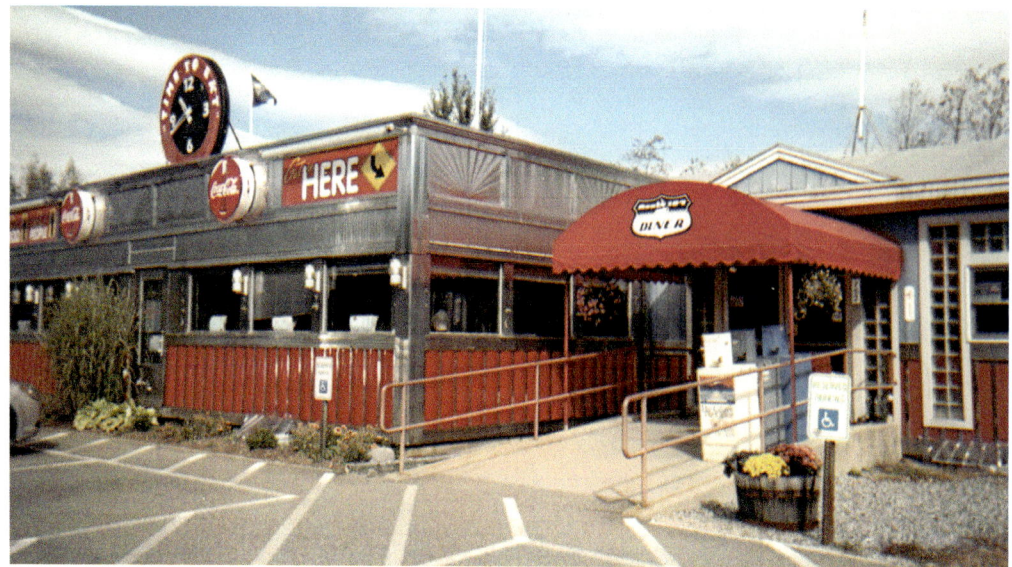

oute 104 Diner (Bobby's Girl) is a Worcester Diner (#850) from 1956. The diner was the last Worcester diner built. After many years the diner closed in 1987. It was restored and moved to its present location in New Hampton, NH. *Photo courtesy of the author*

Signed,
Dustin P.
Santa Monica, CA

February 21, 2010—If you are looking for a great breakfast spot other than a typical Dunkin Donuts, this diner is worth a trip. We've eaten there many times on various trips to the New Hampton School, and it continues to be a spot that combines great service, fun atmosphere, and good food. I highly encourage the "counter", as it's a great way to always keep your coffee mug full. Lunch is always fun there as well, but breakfast is by far the best.

Signed,
Carl L.
Alamo, CA

May 20, 2011—Great place for breakfast, Fun décor. Little pricy when you add in coffee, etc. Nice size servings. Though my veggie omelet had just about an entire onion in it. The home fried were awesome. Service friendly. The sandwiches looked really interesting too. Husband had a stack of pancakes which he devoured. Oh and they have a full liquor license…

Signed,
Christine S.
Reading, MA

Shore Diner was one of the most popular and social magnets of Laconia and the Lakes Region. The diner was a place where you could get a good quick meal, but were welcome to spend as much time as you liked to socialize and gab with your neighbor or a stranger just traveling through and wanted a cup of coffee. Besides the fine food, this diner had the best entertainment, from the wait-staff to the cooks. The highlight was the cook-waiter, Ken Osgood, better known as "Spider." Everyone was fascinated and entertained by watching him attend to his customer with speed you could not imagine. When a customer ordered a cup of coffee from the far end of the counter, he would immediately pour the coffee and would send the cup speeding down to the far end of the counter and stop directly in front of the customer; he seldom missed his target. Believe it or not—he was good.

Everyone felt welcome and it didn't matter how long you stayed as long as you left satisfied with the food, coffee, and service.

The location of the Shore Diner was along Route 3 on the shore of Paugus Bay (Lake Winnipesaukee) in (Lakeport) Laconia, New Hampshire.

Sunny Day Diner is an expanded 1958 Master Diner. It was originally located in Dover, New Jersey, where it was known as "Stoney's Diner." It was moved to Lincoln in 1988 and named "Jay's Sweetheart Diner." It has since been renamed during the late 1990s as the "Sunny Day Diner." The diner is considered to be the only Master diner in Northern New England.

The diner is located on Rte. 3 (Connector Rd.) in Lincoln, NH 03251.

Public Review of the Sunny Day Diner:

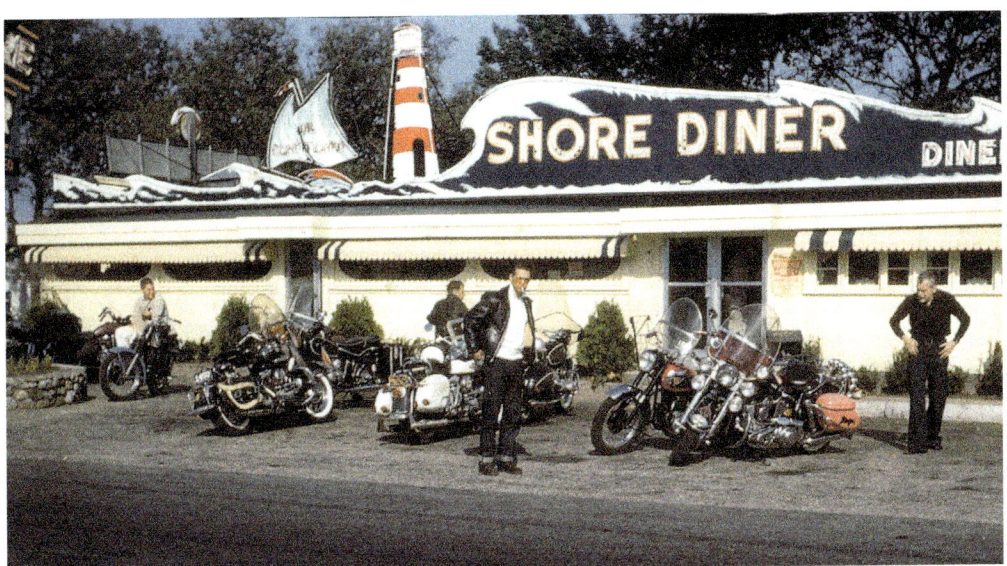

Shore Diner during Motor Cycle Week in June 1961 in Lakeport (Laconia), NH. This diner was a popular eating place, but the entertainment from the cook-waiter was worth the stop. *Photo courtesy of Dan Larson*

On July 11, 2002 a customer by the name Ed Smith wrote the following on the website as an overall rating which is well worth presenting it to a visitor to the North Country:

You understand the meaning of the word serendipity when you come across this wonderful little diner in the White Mountains of New Hampshire. It is a classic diner in every sense. The diner was built by the Master Company of Pequannock, New Jersey. It was originally in Dover, New Jersey before being moved to Lincoln, NH in 1988. It was placed on a full foundation with kitchen addition in the back. In 1997, when the new owners took over the business, they added a complete bakery in the basement. All the meals were prepared from scratch. Nothing overcooked—well prepared with loving care by genuine chefs.

Careful attention is paid to every detail in the presentation of the food and appropriate atmosphere. It is not just a beautiful diner but tastefully restored for the guest's comfort. The diner says 'fun' from the moment you enter the door. This is a diner run by real 'people persons.'

This is a diner worth driving hundreds of mile to visit. The beautiful setting in the White Mountains of New Hampshire isn't a shabby secondary drive goal either. 'Stop by and say hello.'

Signed,
Ed Smith

Tilt'n Diner (C-Man Restaurants), a 1951 O'Mahony Diner, exemplifies the classic décor of the glory days of the 40s and 50s—the juke box, mahogany woodwork, stainless steel sidings, and the long counter with stools line the total length of the diner. The diner offers something for everyone. The Tilt'n Diner is certainly a rebirth for what a New England diner should be like. According to Randy Garbin's *Diners of New England*: "In 1991, the Tilt'n Diner marked a kind of a rebirth for the idea of a diner chain in New England, not seen since the demise of the Monarch Diners in the Boston area during the 1930s to 1960s. The Tilt'n Diner belongs to Alex Ray's Common Man restaurant chain, which has over twelve family-style restaurants spread out between Manchester and Lincoln. The Tilt'n Diner ironically enough, began as a Monarch Diner located in Waltham, Massachusetts. It replaced the first Monarch on that site, a 1940 Worcester now in Lowell operating as the Four Sisters, and later the diner was moved to Salisbury, becoming the Lafayette Diner. In 1939, it was moved to temporary storage in Concord before Alex Ray, owner of the diner, secured its present location in Tilton, NH."

The Diner advertises: "Where our coffee is strong and waitresses are fresh! Complete with be-boppin' music, hearty breakfasts served all day, including the popular 'Cadillac,' and classic comfort food favorites like baked shepherd's pie, and the White Mountain meatloaf."

The Tilt'n Diner opened in 1992 and has been called a "must stop" for the discriminating tourist to the Lakes Region and White Mountains of New Hampshire.

The Tilt'n is located at 61 Laconia Rd, Tilton, New Hampshire exit 20 off I-93 - Tilton, NH 03276.

Public Reviews of the Tilt'n Diner:

February 19, 2013—There are so many great things to choose from but some of our favorites include the Shepherd's Pie . . . meatloaf . . . Reuben . . . sandwich . . . and the classic macaroni and cheese.

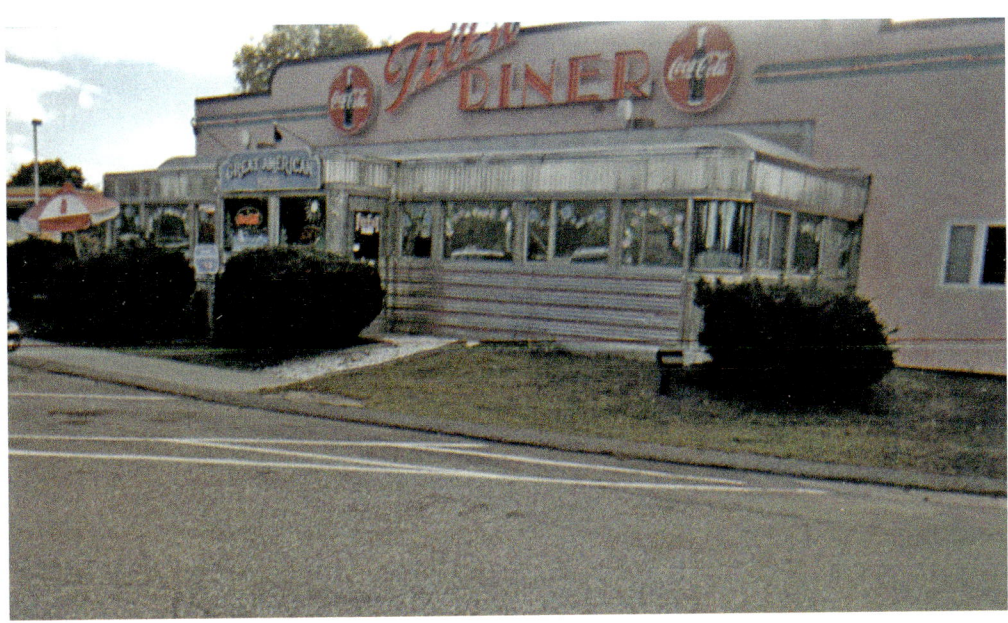

The Tilt 'n Diner is an O'Mahony Diner from 1951. After many years of service in Massachusetts, the diner closed around 1987, and was restored and opened in Tilton, New Hampshire, in 1992. *Photo courtesy of the author*

Pace yourself so that you can save room for dessert because if you think their meals are great then you will LOVE their desserts. The grasshopper pie and toll house pie are always a hit. Enjoy!

Signed,
Cind Pl7

April 18, 2013—The staff at the Tilton Diner are so professional and friendly. I've gone a few times and they never waiver their service or outgoing personalities. Many items to pick from which are all good it's hard to pick. The turkey sandwich with stuffing is so fresh. Salads are equally as fresh and filling. I always go back...

Signed,
Iancates

April 21, 2013—Went to breakfast with the family and it was fun and fabulous—fun and helpful waitress and great food. Great Coffee. The pancakes are awesome, and I am not a huge fan of pancakes! The prices were very reasonable.

Signed,
Hollybloom24

April 22, 2013—It's clean, friendly, look inside nice seats, red everywhere, shiny chrome, old cars in the parking lot, the menu is like the fifties. I like the Philly cheese steak, it was full of onions, peppers, steak, mushrooms, and it's toasted.

Signed,
Tenthouseandshort
Leominster, MA

Union Diner (Paugus Diner) is well known as a neighborhood diner with a friendly atmosphere, and courtesy service. Stop in and enjoy the family cooking.

According to the owners (management), the following history is given:

In 1951, when Worcester Diner car #831 was completed, only 19 more would ever be made. Originally Manus' Diner in Concord, New Hampshire, it suffered a fire and was moved several times before finding its existing home on Union Avenue in Laconia. An addition was completed in 1994 and The Paugus Diner took its place serving good, wholesome, classic food and favorites at realistic prices.

Still mostly preserved, the Union Diner has recently undergone a renovation. We have kept its classic design trademarks that include solid construction and old-fashioned styling that feature oak and mahogany woodwork, intricate ceramic tiled patterns and a back bar of stainless steel. Similar classic lunch car diners fed New England's working class; today, fewer than one hundred lunch cars still operate.

Today, we're here to do whatever is necessary to make you happy and bring you back. We want to be the 'Diner's Diner.' We're proud of our people who help make your visits special and if you are not happy, we want to know about it so we can make it right.

The objectives of the Union Diner are: 1. To serve the highest quality food at the lowest prices possible. 2. To take care of the guests and those who serve them, and 3. The Diner cares about people and wants to do the right thing.

The Union Diner is located at 1331 Union Avenue, Laconia, NH 03246.

Public Reviews of the Union Diner:

November 1, 2012—Great little old school diner! Lobster stew was delicious, not too heavy and seasoned perfectly. Steak tips cooked perfectly too. Burgers, fries, chicken. Everything we had was delicious. Prices were great. Waitress was prompt and personable. I got the Windy City dog with fries. It was a kayem dog. Chicago style with tomatoes, relish, celery salt and hot peppers. Fantastic! We would definitely return.

Signed,
Beth R.
Watertown, MA

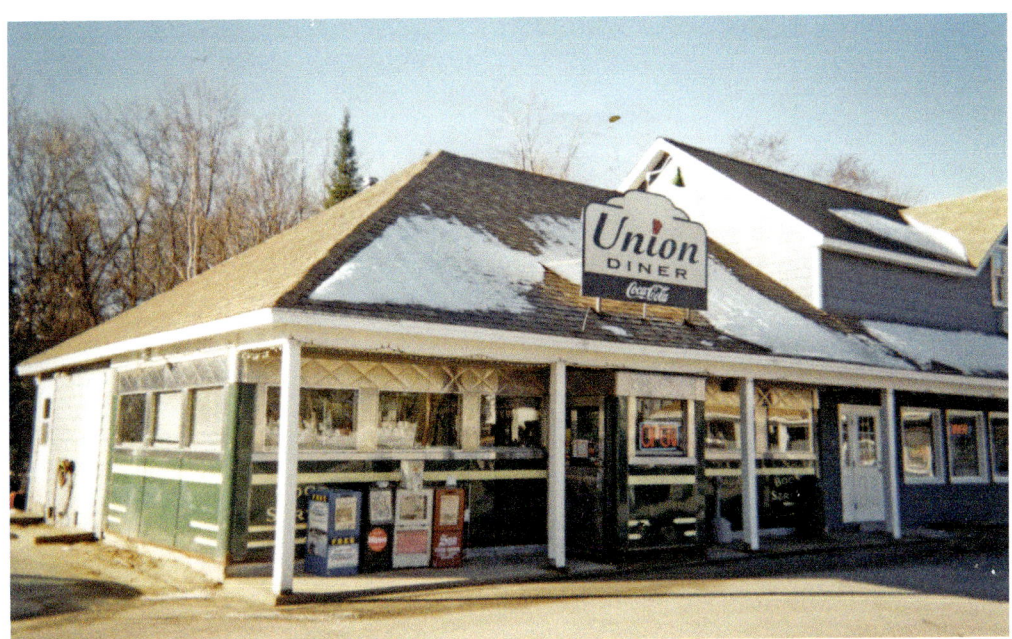

The Union Diner is a Worcester Diner (#831) from 1951. Originally it was known as "Manus Diner" in Concord, NH and moved to Union Avenue and named the "Paugus Diner." The diner suffered from a fire in 1991, but was restored. In 2009, new ownership renamed the diner as the "Union Diner." Located in Lakeport (Laconia), NH. *Courtesy of the author*

October 9, 2011—Good food, great value, no nonsense diner fare. Breakfast for a family is delicious and the best priced options in the area. Service in the morning can be slow and needs improvement, but not a reason to skip the Union. Bus boy has a great attitude and wonderful with kids. Eggs Benedict got thumbs up from all the adults. Youth pancake connoisseur always asks to go back. Went for dinner for the first time recently. All homemade comfort food and excellent. Everyone said they will go back often. Service at night was better, wait staff attentive and knew the food, offered options. Less expensive than going to McDonald's, and yummy, wholesome, diner food.

Signed,
Bl
Beverly Hills, CA

Chapter Six
List of Non-Classic Diners of New Hampshire

Andre's Diner is located off the beaten path in a small strip plaza on Willow Street, Manchester, NH. The diner is located at 100 Willow Street, Manchester, NH 03103.

Public Reviews of Andre's Diner:

February 17, 2010—This place is owned and operated by a friendly woman, who does the short order cooking in the kitchen and serves the customer too. The diner has a cozy feel with a few tables and booths and a small C shaped lunch counter and a good sized kitchen area with grill. The walls are painted sea green colors.

The menu offers the typical breakfast dishes including 18 kinds of omelets on the menu and breakfast specials are offered as well. The prices are pretty reasonable, most omelets served with pan fried and toast.

I finally dined here for the first time this morning on my way to work. I needed to have a good breakfast, but enjoy it very quickly since I had a long day ahead. There were a few customers already here including a group of City Highway Dept. workers. That's a good sign, the food has to be pretty good.

I sat up at the counter for prompt service. I was offered coffee, which was good and on the strong side. I ordered the top Breakfast Special, which included 2 eggs any style, pan fries or beans, bacon and toast. I watched my food being cooked to order on the grill. The breakfast was solid, good and very tasty. The pan fries (fresh cut grilled potatoes) were crispy and browned outside and soft inside. The folded scrambled eggs were soft and fluffy and I put some hot sauce on it for some kick. The bacon strips were crispy, just the way I specified. The wheat toast was already buttered.

The service was pretty good and quick. I was offered more coffee, but I needed to boogie and quickly settle up on the tab. I was in and out in 15 minutes.

I'll definitely be returning to Andre's Diner for the good breakfast, but I'll try to stop in here on my day off.

Signed,
Ian W.
Pelham, NH

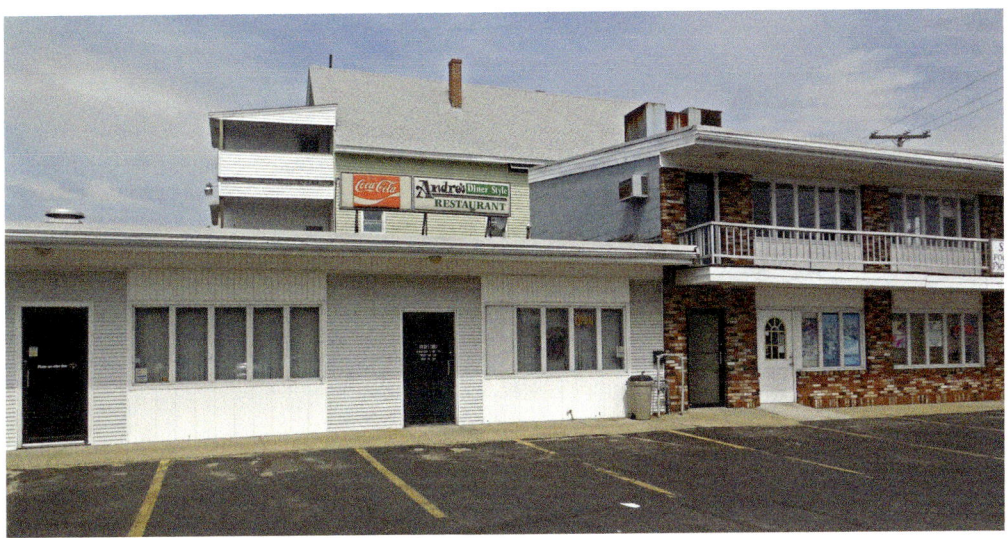

Andre's Diner, Willow Street, Manchester. *Photo courtesy of Ron Scully*

Center Harbor Diner is considered a non-traditional diner (not classic in style), in the heart of the Lakes Region on Lake Winnipesaukee. It appeals to the local clientele—the parking lot is often full.

The Center Harbor Diner is located on 17 Whittier Hwy. Rte. 25, Moultonborough, NH 03254.

Public Review of Center Harbor Diner:

May 9, 2011—Center Harbor Diner is located along a busy stretch of NH 25. The roadside country diner serves up breakfast (all day) and lunch is reasonably priced in a touristy area. The atmosphere inside "no frills" which has counter seating with padded stools and two dining areas with folding tables and folding chairs.

The food served here is home style American country cooking. The breakfast menu offerings include eggs and omelets and served with home fries and toast), pancakes, and French toast which include coffee, plus breakfast sandwiches and breakfast sides.

The lunch menu includes sandwiches, burgers, salad plates, soups, chowder, sides (fries, rings, slaw, cottage cheese, applesauce, fruit cocktail). And comfort dinners (8 oz. steak dinner, chopped sirloin, meatloaf, ham plate, liver & onions, chicken fingers, chicken parmesan). Pepsi products are served here. Daily specials are posted near the counter. The prices are pretty reasonable.

Signed,
Ian W.
Pelham, NH

June 21, 2012—'Nothing beats a great breakfast' . . . was in the area for Motorcycle Week and found Center Harbor on our way out for the day. There were three of us who pretty much "live to eat rather eat to live." Greeted at the door and seated right away, asked if we wanted coffee just the way a diner should. Our waitress was terrific, told us the daily specials and gave us our menus.

I chose the daily special, biscuits and gravy with 3 eggs and toast, the other guys ordered eggs, bacon and ham. We all got side of hash. As for mine the biscuit and gravy was as good as it gets. I love South and could live on grits, biscuits and gravy and country ham. Food came out fast and hot . . . came by several times to refill coffee.

Overall, great meal for the price. Great Service. Highly recommend. . . .

Signed,
Frank B.
Milton, MA

Cote's Diner is a non-traditional diner, but the interior is an appealing classic diner style décor. The diner is located on 1 Pinard Street in Manchester, NH 03102.

Public Review of Cote's Diner:

August 16, 2008—Cote's Diner is the place to go for a cheap good breakfast. The diner serving the Goffstown area for over 40 years is frequented by lots of older locals where everyone knows each other.

The prices are very reasonable and omelets, pancakes, & French toast also come with bottomless coffee. The simple menu offers eggs, port pie, oatmeal, egg sandwiches, BLT, pan fries, beans, meat, toast bagels. Maxwell House coffee, tea, hot chocolate, soda, juices, and milk.

This very casual diner has two sections. The front section is packed small with lunch counter stool seating. The more spacious hack section is the dining room with booth and table seating plus old framed baseball photos on the walls and TV. There's also a bar area with lottery, scratch ticket machine, and dart board too.

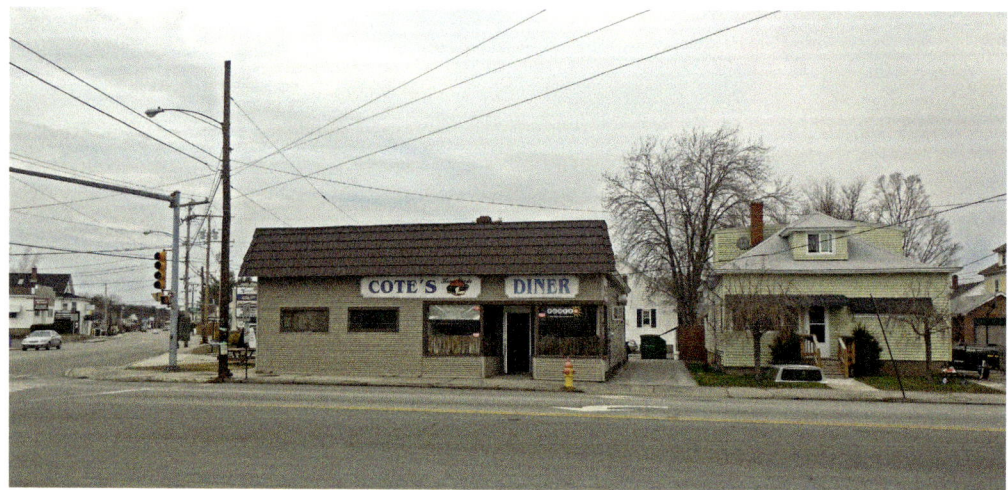

Cote's Diner—a diner frequented by regulars. *Photo courtesy of Ron Scully*

Signed,
Ian W.
Manchester, NH

Derry Diner is a non-traditional diner, which is a fine restaurant located in Derry, New Hampshire. The diner is located at 29 Crystal Avenue Derry, NH 03038–(603) 434-6499.

Public Review of Derry Diner:

May 25, 2007—Open 7 days a week for breakfast and lunch. The Derry Diner offers a basic menu including items such as eggs, omelets, pancakes, French toast, waffles, bacon, sausage, ham, home fries, beans, toast, and muffins. For lunch, sandwiches, burgers, plate specials (ham steak), and desserts are offered.

    This non-smoking diner has a "down home" atmosphere with small framed pictures on the walls and several signs behind the lunch counter (8 stool seats) displaying some good wise proverbs (you'll have to visit the diner to see them) and gray colored seats. There's also booth seating and table seating available. The menus are already at each table.

    NOTE: On the weekends, there is a 2 person minimum to sit at the booths and tables. I had breakfast here recently on a weekend and I sat myself at a booth. I ordered coffee and three breakfast items. The Sunrise Sandwich is an egg substitute with green peppers and onions on multi-grain toast, tasty and light. The Home Fries consisted of grilled potato chunks, which was okay. The Texas French Toast consisting of egg-battered thick bread and topped with cinnamon sugar and powdered sugar which was soft and sweet. The service here was decent with a free refill on coffee and quick delivery of food from the kitchen.

Signed,
Ian W.
Pelham, NH

November 27, 2011—My boyfriend and I have been going here for a little while now so it's a place I definitely know. His father lives in Derry so it's only 5 minutes down the road which makes it pretty convenient. Though this place may not look amazing from the outside, the food is quite decent. Every time I go here, I usually get one of their omelets since I am a huge fan of omelets. Last time I went to the Derry Diner, I got an omelet with black olives, cheddar cheese, and it had other various vegetables in it. I think what I like most about Derry Diner is the fact that everyone there is very nice. The wait to get your food isn't that long and everything I have, even had there has been good. I have never gotten cold food and the only thing I would say isn't amazing is their home fries.

    Unfortunately, both my boyfriend and I have yet to find one place with amazing home-fries so I won't penalize them there. One thing I will say stinks is that in the summer time they put their air conditioner on, so it gets so cold inside I'm practically freezing. Also know that it gets VERY busy during the weekends so I would recommend getting there early.

Signed,

Ver C.
Newburyport, MA

Donna Jean's Diner: "Never Trust a Skinny Cook," seems to be a feature comment from a very popular diner at The Weirs.

The location of Donna Jean's is 1208 Weirs Blvd. (near The Weirs bridge and roundabout), Laconia, NH 03246.

Public Review of Donna Jean's Diner:

June 14, 2009—We go to Donna Jean's at least once a weekend during early summer then we switch to another place that is a little closer to the Mountain View Yacht Club, where we have a boat.

Donna Jean's is exceptionally well run and clean, and Donna Jean's is always on site making sure everything goes smoothly. The servers do an excellent job of making sure orders are taken and delivered promptly and coffee cups never go empty.

The food is fairly typical of a diner-type restaurant, and it is always well prepared and tasty. Be sure to try a free sample of their homemade baked beans—great with breakfast!

Signed,
Sandy H.
Hollis, NH

May 4, 2012—We stopped here two days in a row for breakfast. We were visiting the region with friends & it has become their go-to breakfast spot when in the area. For the most part standard diner food. Everyone enjoyed their meals, though on day 1 I ordered the breakfast burrito & did not think it was very special. Day 2 however, I ordered the same as my friend the "Winnisquam" version of their variety of eggs benedict dishes—totally changed my mind about the place. With that one dish I went from "meh, it's ok" to "I want this for breakfast every time we are in Laconia." So, this totally strikes me as an YMMV place, depending on your personal taste.

Signed,
Laura H.
Leominster, MA

August 9, 2012—We visited here yesterday, and it was incredibly good! We had an omelet with raisin toast and home fries, and the "Pigs in a Blanket" special (sausage wrapped in pancakes), with home fries. We also had coffee and mimosas. Everything was very tasty, and the pancakes weren't heavy. The coffee was fresh and the mimosas were made perfectly, great addition to our meals. The service was excellent, too! All of the staff were very friendly. Also, they offered a side of "real" NH maple syrup, so if you're into that, it's a great ADDITION TO THE MEAL!

Signed,
Kristy L.
West Bridgewater, MA

February 27, 2013—On a recent trip to the Lakes Region, I needed a cup of coffee, ASAP! I actually also needed breakfast since we all know that breakfast is the meal of champions. On my way through Weirs Beach, I have passed a small diner dozens of times and had never stopped. Huge mistake on my part.

    We were able to be seated right away. I didn't count the number of tables, but I bet the diner could hold 80–100 people (don't quote me on that). There are tables that look out over the channel and if you were fortunate to sit at one of those window seats, you would be able to watch the boats go by. I am hoping to sit at one of those tables on my next visit. The diner is quaint, comfortable, and relaxed. I loved a couple of the signs that were hanging on the wall: "Never trust a skinny cook" and my favorite, "This is a drama-free zone!"

    Our waitress, Tori greeted us with a smile and a cup of coffee, brewed to perfection. The veggies in my vegetable scramble were cooked just right: not too mushy and not too crisp. My husband chose the ham-and-cheese omelet and he truly enjoyed each bite. We are both picky about our hash browns, so the question was, would Donna Jean's hash brown pass the test? I am happy to report that they were cooked to perfection.

    Nothing like a delicious filling breakfast to start my day! Bon Appetite!

Signed,
Debby Kelley
Londonderry, NH

George's Diner was opened by its present owners Roger and Robin Rist in May 1991. The basic philosophy--that fresh and simple ingredients make the best meals possible leads to the motto "Just Good Food."

    They enjoy their long-term relationship with employees and customers. The staff strive for quality and consistency in the preparation and serving of their home-cooked food.

    Whether it be made-to-order breakfasts, quick turn-around lunch specials or more leisurely dinner specials followed by homemade desserts, they hope you enjoy your meal.

    Note: Before the diner was named "George's," it was known as the "Musher's Den."

    The diner is located at 10 Plymouth St. in Meredith, New Hampshire, just a short walk from the Town Docks on Lake Winnipesaukee.

Public Reviews of George's Diner:

May 7, 2013—I'm a frequent diner at George's. I always feel I'm getting good value and food. There has been a few misses in not so great lunch specials, but more often than not, it's quite good. Very good fried seafood, excellent Reuben sandwich, breakfast is always good. The only food I stay away from is the chicken and pork dishes…

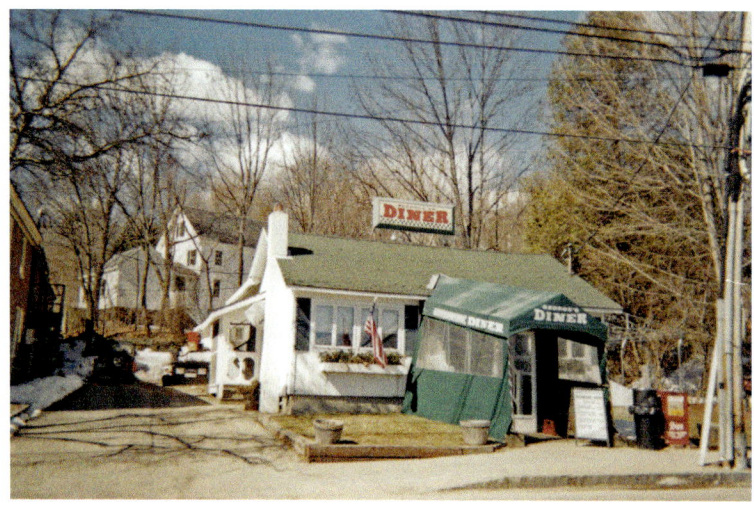

George's Diner, Meredith, NH. I enjoy breakfast at George's Diner quite often and I recommend it to the hungry traveler. *Photo courtesy of the author.*

Signed,
Rthiker 540
Nashua, NH.

March 5, 2013—Almost always crowded so get there early. The local fare such as Shepherd's pie, chicken pot pie, and their baked beans are outstanding! One of my wonderful experiences was a cheeseburger omelet! Always interesting and delicious specials. Order their specials. They run out.

Signed,
Jan A.
Plymouth, NH.

February 1, 2013—If you want a meal in a place that reminds you of home-cooked meals, this is it. Great for breakfast, but we have been there for lunch and it was very good as well. Busy place, but in the summer months they do have a covered dining outside.

Signed,
Sandmolake
Alton Bay, NH.

October 20, 2012—Travelling from England, we knew we were in America when we entered the diner. Good basic US food, plenty of choices, large helpings and friendly staff. A pleasant change from the nearby hotel facilities.
Signed,
Customer.

Margie's Dream Diner is located at 172 Hayward Street, Manchester, NH 03103.

Public Review for Margie's Dream Diner:

July 30, 2011—Go here. Now! Seriously. Do your belly a favor. We are still full from the generous portions of breakfast this morning. Egg Benedict was simply incredible! Super amazing diner with a friendly mom and pop atmosphere. Husband and wife own and run this place lovingly, making everything from scratch. We will most definitely visit this place again—as soon as possible! Everything on the menu looked divine. I was blown away by the owners knew people by name as they walked in. Clearly, this place has loyal eaters for a reason.

Signed,
Amy D.
Manchester, NH

June 28, 2012—I hesitate to give a glowing review for fear that more people will find this place . . . and then I'll never be able to get a seat there again. In all fairness, I can only review breakfast, but that's why you go to a diner anyway, isn't it? My husband and I had a late breakfast there yesterday. I ordered the cheese omelet, he had the veggie omelet. SOOOOO good, the food was hot, the coffee refilled without asking, the table was spotless.

What really impressed me were the choices. Most diners serve fried potatoes—I hesitate to call them home fries because New Hampshire tend to think any potato cubed and deep fried is a home fry—but Margie's Dream also offers REAL hash browns and REAL (2 per portion!) potato pancakes. Both options were nicely seasoned brown, crispy bits of heaven! YUM! The eggs were hot, light and moist. We also had a choice of toast, English muffin, or biscuit—which was buttered and grilled—or beans. How could you not like having breakfast there? We left satisfied and planning our next visit.

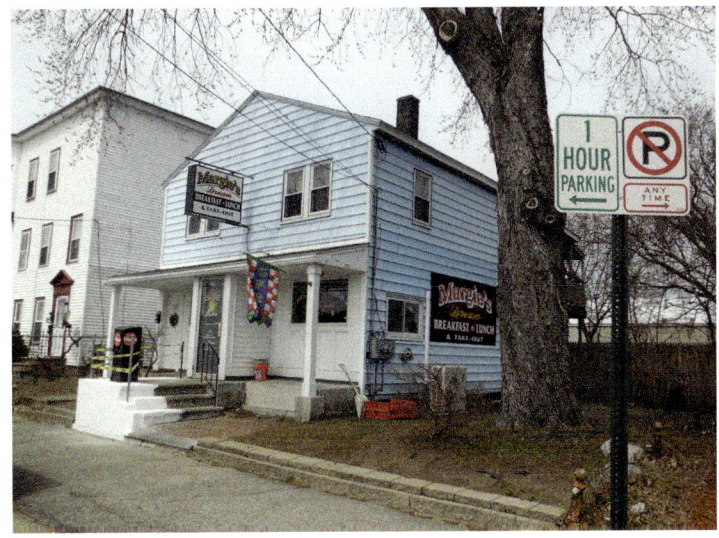

Margie's—where everybody knows everybody, every day.
Photo courtesy of Ron Scully

Signed,
Bridget P.
Londonderry, NH

January 2, 2013—A friend of ours recommended the diner this summer. We now go about twice a month and we usually go on a weekday around 9 a.m. Parking isn't an issue at that time, but we have had other visits since when it is. I usually run inside to make sure we can get a booth—as seating is pretty limited—Maybe about 30 seats (We have two young children that can't sit at the counter).

It's our favorite diner in town; they even had scrapple as a special once! The food is always perfectly cooked, and the wait isn't long, even if the restaurant is packed. The selection has something for everyone. We haven't tried lunch because the breakfast items are just too good. I highly recommend the skillets, though I usually get the breakfast sandwich because there is so much food on the skillet. My children share a chocolate chip pancake and an order of bacon. We LOVE the waitress—she's an asset to the restaurant and perfect at her job. I highly recommend this place to all of my friends.

Market Place Diner is not a classic-looking diner on the exterior; however, the interior is considered a typical diner style. The diner is considered that "hidden restaurant" and has yet to be reviewed, but is considered to be a diner of interest.

The Market Place Diner is located at 4 Village Market Place, Hollis, NH 03049.

Public Review for Market Place Diner:

January 13, 2012—I grew up in Hollis, and have many fond memories of this diner. Friendly staff and always accommodating. I love to go out to breakfast with my parents when I am back in town and always opt for this diner or Country Kitchen. Marketplace Diner also has dinner and lunch, and staff were nice enough to find out all ingredients to be sure my meal was vegetarian.

Signed,
LaParadiddle
Boston, MA

April 19, 2010—The lobster Benedict is just to die for. Mike (owner) will whip up and breakfast combo that your heart desires. Vinnie's homemade hash has a hint of heat that matches up perfectly with poached eggs and toast.
Signed,
DPB
Brookline, NH

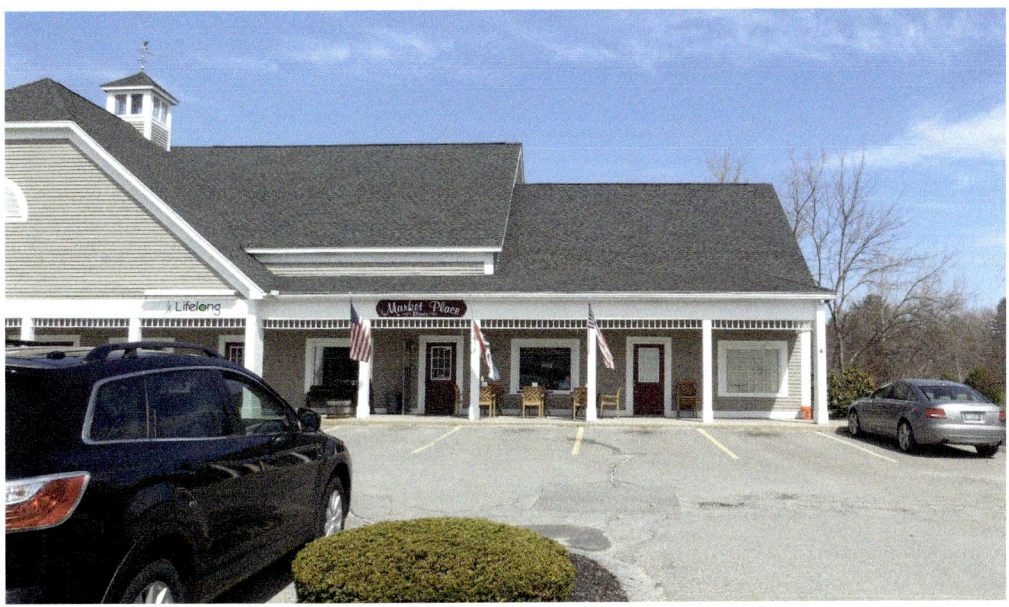

Exterior of the Market Place Diner. *Photo courtesy of Ron Scully*

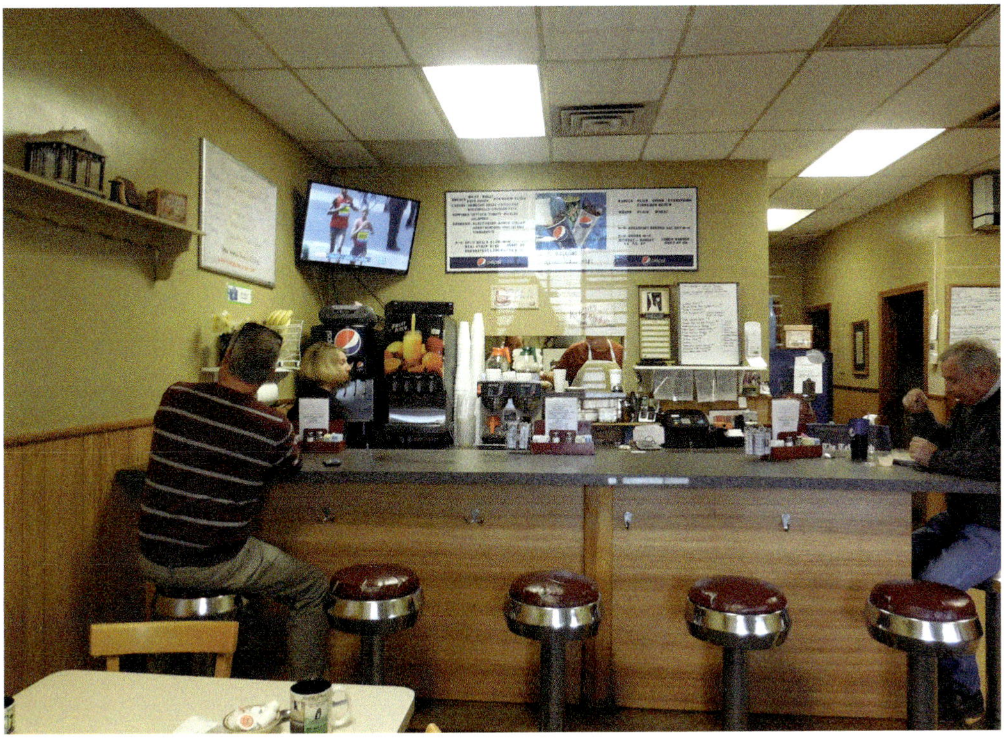

Original diner stools inside the Market Place Diner. *Photo courtesy of Ron Scully*

Pink Cadillac Diner is a family style diner with a 1950s theme including old fashioned jukeboxes and a black and white checkered floor. Breakfast, lunch and dinner are served every day of the week.

The diner is located at (Rte. 11) 17 Farmington Rd., Rochester, NH 03867.

Public Reviews for Pink Cadillac Diner:

November 5, 2012—'Perfect American diner with more than perfect fins.' If you're a tourist, like we are, then diners have a peculiar attraction. They're a kind of direct contact with the mythical America we feel we know from the movies, the pink Cadillac ticks all the boxes, it has a pink Cadillac instead of an awning outside, secondly it's homey inside thirdly, the staff of this family run....

Signed,
Zoltan56
Newcastle on tyne

August 6, 2011—Wow—Love this place!

Signed,
Jeanneinmaine
Acton, Maine.

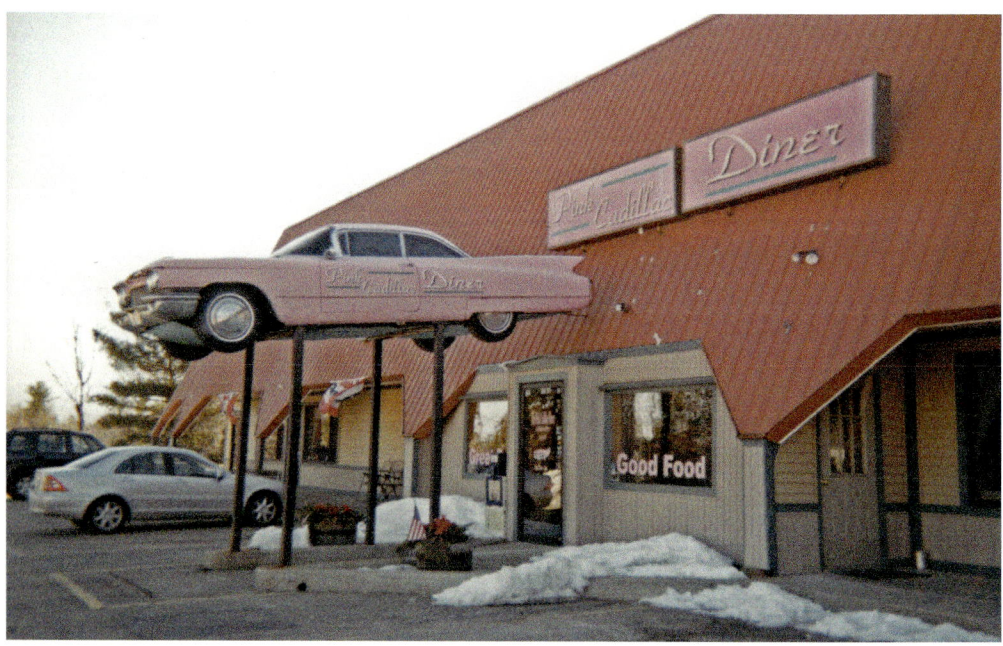

The Pink Cadillac, Rochester, NH. Flying high over the entrance to the diner is the Pink Cadillac in its full glory of the '50s. The food is fine – it's worth the stop. *Photo courtesy of The author*

List of Non-Classic Diners of New Hampshire

The Swanzey Diner is located at 515 Monadnock Hwy 11, Swanzey, NH 03446.

Public Reviews of Swanzey Diner:

June 26, 2010—I stopped at this little country restaurant for lunch. The parking looked almost full around noontime on a Saturday from the outside, which is a great sign that the food at the Swanzey Diner must be pretty good. They serve breakfast (served until 11:30 a.m.), lunch and dinner (Wed–Saturday).

Once inside I glanced over the specials board and then found an open table in the corner of the very cozy dining room, which has several booths and finished wood trim wall and with signs of various towns in SW NH. The waitress promptly took my drink order while I went over the menu. Some of the lunch/dinner offerings included grilled sandwiches burgers. Melts, Clubs, wraps, salads pasta, comfort dishes (liver & onions, port, pot roast, ham steak), fried and grilled chicken, fresh seafood, (scallops, shrimps, haddock, clams), and desserts (ice cream, pies, shortcake, pineapple upside down cake). The prices are pretty fair, most items (except seafood), under $10.

I went with the Gobblers served with natural fried chips, and a dill pickle slice. The grill sandwich was very good and served very hot with oven roasted turkey, crisp bacon, melted Swiss, and tomatoes on grills Texas toast (lots of butter). The side of cranberry mayo was a rich touch. The chips were lightly salted and crispy. I 'gobbled' up my lunch quickly. The service was prompt, especially during a busy lunch. The staff here were also carrying on several conversations with the regular customers (by first name).

Overall, a great lasting lunch for under $10.

Signed,
Ian W.
Pelham, NH

December 22, 2010—Great little diner recommended to be by a local merchant so that says something. Had a mid-day meal here after the Currier and Ives Tour in December. First time in Swanzey as well. The service was prompt, the server was quite courteous and efficient, and the meal was worthwhile and hit the spot and very reasonably priced. I ordered salad and a bowl of their New England clam chowder. Would definitely return to this establishment, when in the vicinity.

Signed,
Brenda B.
Fitchburg, MA

Wolfeborough Diner is located in the center of the village near the bridge, and across the street is Wolfeborough Bay, Lake Winnipesaukee. The location is ultra-convenient. The diner is rather small, but cozy and friendly. It is not your typical classic diner, however, when you enter the establishment you find yourself in a diner atmosphere. Don't expect to park right in front if it is the middle of the summer. The diner is small, with a counter with swivel stools, three large booths in the middle, which can hold six people and four or five four-person booths. If it is tourist season, expect to wait, but it usually isn't too long. It's a diner after all and turn around is fast. If you are in there and there is waiting, please be polite and don't dally when you are done!

The Wolfeborough Diner is located at 5 North Main Street, Wolfeboro, NH 03894.

Public Review of The Wolfeborough Diner:

> March 20, 2013—Locals just call it 'the diner.' The only diner in town, but the only one you need. It's amazing to find omelets done so perfectly thin at a little local hole-in-the-wall. They have a variety of Eggs Benedict including my personal favorite—Eggs Blackstone, which substitutes tomato and bacon for the ham—fabulous! The only downside on the menu for us hash brown lovers is the oval-shaped hash brown patties. However, it isn't a deal breaker even for me and I go there often with my kind. The portion sizes are generous enough to satisfy even my teenage son the options enough to satisfy my picky teenage daughter. Waffles, pancakes, chicken-fried steak, breakfast sandwiches. Want lunch? They have a full lunch menu with melts and burgers- you want it, you got it. Diner food at all its best. One caveat for Jersey folks; I have yet to see a Freddy (Taylor Ham/Pork Roll) sandwich on the menu.
>
> Signed,
> A satisfied customer

Special Note: The Yankee Flyer Diner is a very attractive mural of a diner which held a prominent spot in the City of Nashua. This mural, located in the same spot as the original diner, depicts life in the city during the 1940s and '50s. The mural shows a number of Nashua locals from that time period. Until the diner was sold and moved in 1965, the diner was the place to eat and socialize.

A plaque located next to the mural provides details about the mural and the individuals whose faces help give the mural its charm and character.

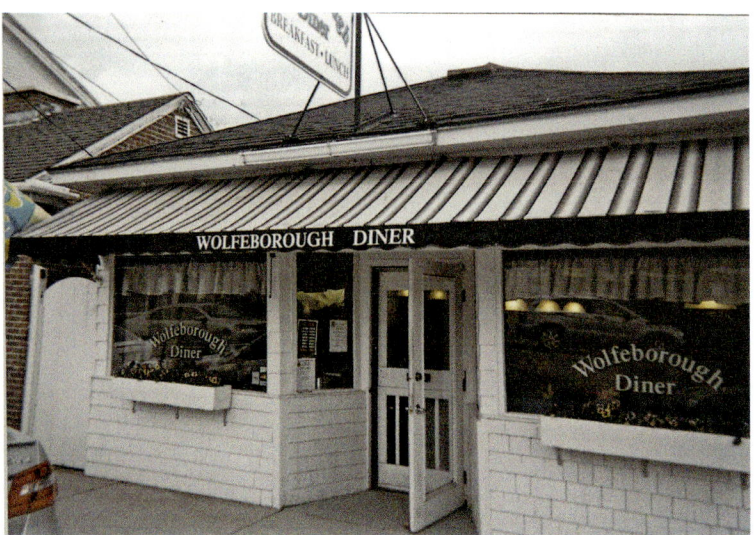

Wolfeborough Diner, Main St. Wolfeborough, NH. Located in the village by the bridge and the docks of Lake Winnipesaukee is a small but satisfying diner with fine food for the family. *Photo courtesy of the author.*

Chapter Seven
Railroad Diners

The Café Lafayette Dinner Train

Lincoln, New Hampshire 93251
According to Lance Burak and Leslie Holloway, owners of Café Lafayette Dinner Train, it has been in operation since 1989.

The guest is welcomed to relax and be comfortable with the rhythm of the rails to enjoy your expectations of a vintage train ride. Seated in the train's beautifully restored car, the guest may totally enjoys the views of New Hampshire scenery, i.e., the mountains, mountain streams, and when riding in the dining car a five-course meal and impeccable served by friendly servers so as to enjoy the every changing scenery.

According to the owners, the following history is given:

There are about 20 moving dinner trains in all of North America, making The Café Lafayette Dinner Train a very unique attraction in the Lincoln and North Woodstock area.

The 'Granite Eagle' was originally built for the Missouri-Pacific Railroad, operating from St. Louis Missouri to San Antonio Texas in the mid-1950s on the 'Texas Eagle.' She was then acquired by the Illinois Central RR and run on train #1, 'The City of New Orleans.' The unusual dome car was purchased in Pittsburg Kansas in the late fall of 1995. It was brought across the United States by rail and refurbished in the engine house of the Hobo Railroad during the winter of 1996. Leslie, Lance and their two chefs, Doug Trulson and Scott Buckland along with a friend Tom Sabourn, made the impossible happen; taking only six months to rebuild exterior steel, design and restore the interior, install new windows, and give this magnificent car a royal blue and white paint job, then renaming her the 'Granite Eagle.'

The Indian Waters #221 dining car is a beautifully restored 1924 Pullman dining car originally built for the New York Central Railroad. The car was rebuilt from the trucks up in the Winnipesaukee Rail Yard by skilled craftsman and the previous owner in the mid-1980s. It operated for two years on the Winnipesaukee Railroad and was moved to Lincoln in the summer of 1988. It then operated for one year on the Hobo Railroad before it was purchased by the current owners, Lance and Leslie Holloway. They continued to operate the 'Indian Waters' from the rail station until the summer of 1998 when the Café Lafayette Dinner Train was moved to the new location at the 'Eagle's Nest.' Due to the age of the 'Indian Waters,' she is not used on a regular basis.

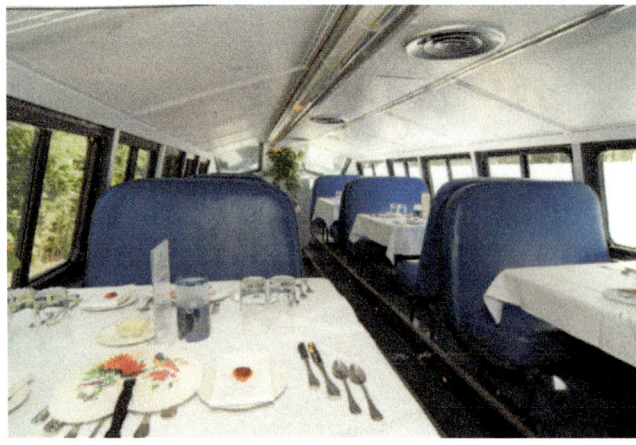

Lafayette Dinner Train interior Dome dining room, Lincoln, NH. The Café Lafayette is where you want to be when you visit and dine, for an enjoyable ride through the White Mountain landscape. *Courtesy of Hobo Railroad.*

Public Reviews of Café Lafayette Dinner Train:

March 24, 2013—My parents gave me the best birthday ever in July 2012, with a trip on the dinner train. It was truly incredible dining experience! The entire meal was on par with the finest restaurants in the country and the service was tremendous! Our server, David (now is the head waiter, according to a special on Great Scenic Railway Journeys), really knew how to make us feel special. He was charming, funny, and perfectively attentive. I love when a server really gets into their role and the dining experience becomes a living experience. We had seats in the dome of the 'Granite Eagle' train. It was beautifully appointed, with amazing view of the river, meadows, and mountains. My first course included delicious scallops and salad. For the main course, I had the filet mignon, served with mashed potatoes. It was all perfectly cooked and so, so, so scrumptious! I forgot now what the desserts were, but I remember we enjoyed them!

My parents surprised me with a birthday cake that the chef also made on special order. It included white cake with strawberries, my favorite! One of my parents ordered the salmon with the multi-grain pilaf. And it looked delicious, as well. They also have a full bar and I got to order my favorite drink, gin and tonic with Bombay Sapphire. I can't say enough good things about the Café Lafayette Dinner train. If you love trains, beautiful scenery, amazing food and dessert, a classy atmosphere, and wonderful service, you will LOVE this dining experience!

Signed,
Amber K.
North Hollywood, CA

October 14, 2011—I would give a rating of 10 stars if it was possible. This was the BEST experience especially during fall foliage season. The staff was extremely professional and made sure that everything was done to everyone's liking. All of the five courses were to the highest standards and they offered a few choices for the appetizers and entrees. The service was top notch with perfect timing between the courses, not too early and not waiting either with big band jazz music playing in the overhead speakers giving an incredible relaxed ambiance and made a perfect evening. I will definitely do it again anytime I am in the area. This is a must do for anyone that wants to enhance their experience to the Franconia Notch area.

Signed,
Marc P.
Escondido, CA

The Conway Scenic Railroad & Dining Car "Chocorua"

North Conway, New Hampshire 03860

Conway Scenic Railroad delights in being an old-fashioned railroad experience on vintage trains that all depart from the 1874 Victorian station near the common in the village of North Conway. The railroad company is a step back in time which the entire family will enjoy the scenic beauty in the heart of the White Mountains.

The trains are powered by diesel electric locomotives, and by their self-propelled Budd Rail Diesel Car. During the fall foliage season, their popular steam locomotive (#7470) is provided for the North Conway to Conway excursions.

The passenger station was designed by Nathaniel J. Bradlee, and is considered the centerpiece of the rail complex with its most striking edifice in the center of the village.

The station was constructed in 1874 in a Russo-Victorian style. This location is a perfect setting for a ride through the White Mountain National Forest and a perfect view of the Presidential Range. The excursion begins from the depot in North Conway, and travels through the White Mountains via Crawford Notch to Fabyan's Station, Mount Washington and the Cog Railway.

Let us travel aboard the elegant Dining Car "Chocorua" on a delightful excursion through the White Mountains. The following history of the dining car is well presented by the Conway Scenic Railroad Company:

Relive the Golden Days of Railroading

The dining car 'Chocorua,' built by the Pullman Company in 1929, offers a First Class dining experience, complete with friendly and attentive service, in a beautiful oak-paneled restaurant on wheels where the views are constantly changing.

All meals are prepared on board to your order and served with warm, friendly Yankee hospitality. The 'Chocorua' is climate controlled, has a full liquor license, a complete wine list, and is a smoke-free environment.

With advance notice, special dietary needs can be easily accommodated. In the true spirit and tradition of railroad dining, you may be seated at tables of four with other Dining Car guests.

Dining on the rails is a tradition dating back to the mid-to-late nineteenth century, when railroads across the country began offering meal service as an alternative to the roadhouses that were located at their water stops. As competition among the railroads increased, dining car service was taken to new levels, and today, a fascination with this tradition continues.

The location of the Railroad Station is on Main St. No. Conway, New Hampshire.

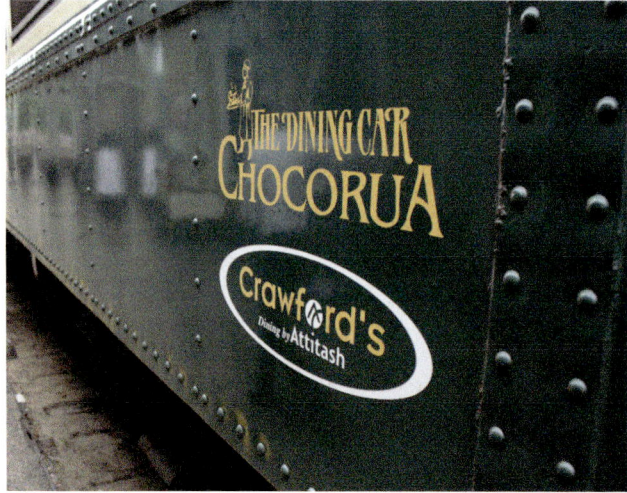

The Chocorua dining car. *Photo courtesy of Conway Scenic Railroad*

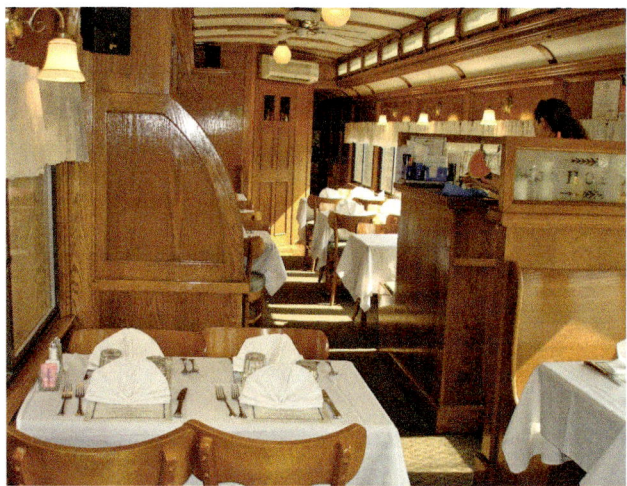

A warm inviting interior. *Photo courtesy of Conway Scenic Railroad*

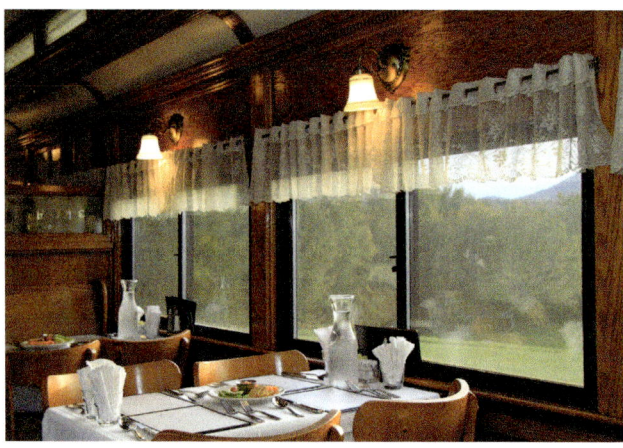

A table with a view. *Photo courtesy of Conway Scenic Railroad*

Public Review for Conway Scenic Railroad:

October 9, 2010—Anyone having the chance to take in this most beautiful experience shouldn't miss it. This is a train trip through some of the most beautiful country that the New England area has to offer, especially during the fall foliage season as we did, the mountains are so beautiful. The rail line personnel are all very professional and a delight to travel with, the rail cars are all restored and kept in excellent condition.

We chose to have lunch in the dining car, which in itself was beautifully restored and most comfortable. The meal was very good and felt the extra was well worth the cost.
We are looking forward to our next rail excursion, wonder if they run a snow train?

Signed,
E. A. MULLER
NEWFIELDS, NH.

Hobo Railroad

64 Railroad Street, Lincoln, NH 03251

Public Reviews of the Hobo Railroad:

May 7, 2013—While traveling through New England, I took my father (total train nut) and he absolutely loved the experience. You don't get to see that many awe inspiring sights but it is a great day trip. The lunch offered on the train was surprisingly very good. It only takes about an hour or so but worth it!

Signed,
Rev Jacob

December 6, 2012—"Polar Express—Lincoln 2012"—We had a wonderful experience with the Polar Express out of Lincoln. An earlier review concerned me but our experience was great. The train was nicely decorated, the staff and volunteers were wonderful, the 'North Pole' was picturesque without buildings including Santa's Workshop and the North Pole Office. Santa worked the whole theatre and our kids were enchanted!

January 11, 2013—"Polar Express on the Hobo Railroad"—This was an amazing experience—for both the kid and the adults! What a great surprise when we arrived at the North Pole and were greeted by so many elves! I can't believe all the nice touches they added. I have done the Polar Express elsewhere, didn't even come close to what we experienced here. It was magical.

Signed,
Colleen W.
Mansfield, MA

Chapter Eight

Reminiscences of the Diner

Richard Gutman—A Life Devoted to the American Diner

Richard Gutman is an expert in American diner history. It is not surprising that someone who spends many hours visiting, eating, talking and writing about them would be anything less than an authority of the diners.

He enters the class diner conundrum and asks himself, "should I have a hamburger or meatloaf for lunch" The aroma of the diner is not complete without the scent of grease-and-coffee air, for this is what make the diner complete. "Breakfast would be nice." He orders one of the most exotic daily specials, a fresh fruit and mascarpone crepe, garnished with a purple orchard. This is not our typical special, but times are changing. Before he takes his first bite, it is his custom to take a picture of the dish and add it to his collection, which number more than 14,000 diner-related images. He speaks proudly that his home is in Boston with his family and his kitchen is designed in the diner-style, with the necessary marble counter, three stools and a menu board all salvages from a 1940s Michigan diner, decorated with several antique pieces from local shops in New Hampshire. I would have thought that he would have chosen a Worcester or an O'Mahony diner being from Massachusetts.

According to Sarah Saffian, a writer for *The Americana*, a Smithsonian magazine, the following is a biographical sketch of his celebration of the diner:

Richard Gutman has been the head of Johnson & Wales University's Art Museum in Providence and the director and curator since 2005. The museum hosts more the 300,000 items, a library of 60,000 volumes and a 25,000 square-foot gallery, featuring a reconstructed 1800s stagecoach tavern, a country of fair displays, a chronology of stove, memorabilia from White House dinners and more. But it's the 4,000-square-foot exhibit, 'Diners: Still Cookin' in the 21st Century,' that is Gutman's labor of love. Indeed, 250 items came from his own personal collection—archival photographs of streamlined stainless steel diners and the visionaries who designed them, their handwritten note and floor plans, class white mugs from the Depression-era, Hotel Diner in Worcester, Massachusetts, 77-year-old lunch wagon wheels, a 1946 cashier's booth. 'It's just one slice of the food service business that we interpret here,' Gutman likes to say, but the diner exhibit is clearly the museum's highlights.

It was in 1872 that Walter Scott introduced the first horse-drawn diner called the night lunch wagon, for it came on at night to cater to the hungry men working in the factories, mills or train stations. The restaurants were closed, so the workers would get their food from a wagon's window and eat sitting on the curb. The diner soon became popular and evolved into a rolling restaurant with a few seats added inside the wagon. It was in 1887 that Samuel Jones respectfully called them lunch cars. Later in 1924, they were known as dining cars. 'If you go to a diner, it's a quick experience,' Gutman explains, 'but it is not an anonymous experience.'

This distinctive sense of community is captured by Richard Gutman when he recalls the ordinary person's story. 'Without the ordinary people, how would the world run? Politicians have to go to diner to connect. What's the word on the street? In diners, you get people from all walks of life, a real cross-section.' And while any menu around the country can be counted on the staples like ham and eggs and meatloaf and asparagus on toast—a region's local flavor is also represented by its diners' cuisine, scrod in New England and crab coast from the sea coast. We must remember that changing times are reflected on the diner menu. What is available in the local farm market of New Hampshire would certainly be on the menu.

If the essential diner is maintained in the midst of change, Richard Gutman would probably approve. But purist that he is, would gladly call our changes that don't pass muster. Diners with Kitsch, games, gumball machines or other junk would certainly frustrate Richard. 'You don't need that kind of stuff in a diner. You don't go there to be transported into an arcade! You go there to be served some good food, and to eat.'

And there you have the simplest definition of what, exactly, this iconic American eatery is. 'It's a friendly place, usually mom-and pop were the sole proprietors, that served the basic home-cooked fresh food for a good value,' Gutman explains. 'In my old age, I've become less of a diner snob, which I think is a good thing.'

Richard is a class act. 'He is generous with his time and knowledge of the roadside delights to all that ask. He has guided myself and others down the road less traveled. We will never know how many diners have been saved because of Richard efforts. Smithsonian has presented a wonderful portrait of a man who saved diners also preserved a living piece of history. Unlike so many museums and historic sites, diners allow us to step back in time and like the old New Hampshire Store, actually experience the taste & smell of our past.

On the morning of July 2, 2010, Bob Williams wrote the following about Richard Gutman:

The Smithsonian has picked the perfect article on such a place as the American Diner. Long before something called Food Network ever ran on cable television, Richard Gutman had logged the miles, eaten more plates of pancakes, waffles and eggs, drank more cups of coffee, and met more owners and customers alike—to learn the lore and culture of the American Diner.

The Smithsonian article captures the diner and Gutman's own perspective very well—and could have been subtitled 'American Diners: Coming Right Up!' Diners may be disappearing, but thankfully the knowledge, photos, and research is safe and intact in the Richard Gutman's own books and archives dedicated to the subject. A second helping on Richard Gutman and diners would be welcome.

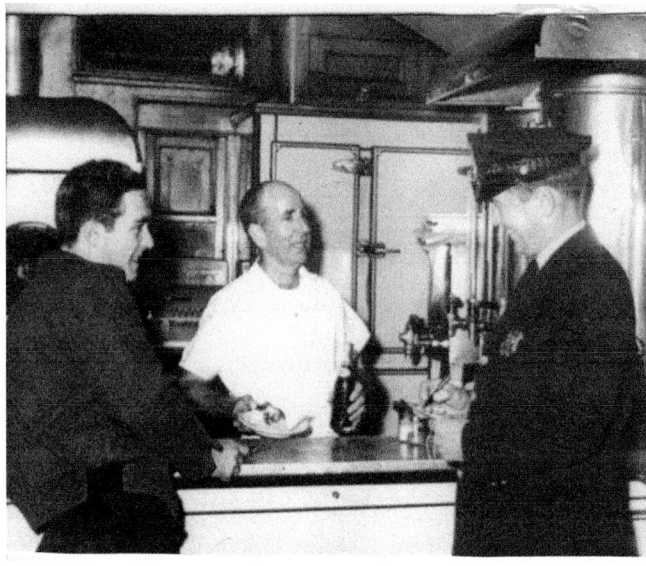

L–R: Walter Gilbert 'Gilley", a guest, and a policeman. Gilley's Diner in Portsmouth, NH. *Courtesy of Stephen and Gina Kennedy.*

Gilley's Back on the Square—Dog Cart Landmark In City, by Bruce Fuller

Portsmouth Herald Staff Writer (2 August 1967)

'If there is anybody in Portsmouth who can be called indispensable,' a local man observed, 'Gilley is the one. He's Portsmouth's indispensable man.'

Walter Gilbert is just an ordinary man. A short, thin, ruddy-faced Irishman with balding gray hair and blue eyes, he is not physically outstanding. He holds no metals or citations. Yet, anyone who has been in Portsmouth for any length of time since 1920s is sure to know 'Gilley.'

One week, Gilley was missing from Market Square for the first time in five years, He seldom, if ever, takes a vacation. Rumors developed that Portsmouth's indispensable man was sick and the city's nocturnal institution would never open for business again.

But Gilley returned after a mild sickness, and his 11 red swivel stools and sliding white door squeaked with the coming and going of customers all night. The word got around fast. Gilley was back in the Square!

Every evening, except for Monday nights, Gilley and his long, red and white dining car pulled up into Market Square for business until the wee hours of the morning.

'Gimme two-dogs with the works and a plate of beans Gil.'

'Hey, Gilley, How'd to Red Sox do yesterday' Think this is their year?'

'Gil, where was that fire down here last night?'

Throughout the night, Gilley's regulars and others come in for food and to chew the fat. Teenagers drop by for a hot dog and hamburger after a date. Patrolmen stop by for a coffee break. Tourists pull up in curiosity. And, during this time, more than 500 of the Gilley's hot dogs fill empty stomachs.

'We've fed generations here as they've come along in the last fifty years,' Gilley remarks from behind the counter of his diner. 'We meet them in school, then in high school, and then pretty soon their kids are coming here.'

'Boys come home to Portsmouth and they always come here and ask, 'Have you heard from this guy, Gil,' or 'Do you know what so-and-so is doing now?''

Gilley knows them all. He admits that he seldom remembers names, but can always remember faces. Everyone is 'Joy' or 'chief' to the Irishman. But they remember him.

Today's dog cart, built in 1940 by the Worcester Diner Co., sits where other lunch carts have done business since the mid-1800s.

Two horse-drawn wagons, one run by Frank Leary and Leo Smith, and the other owned by Gilley's late boss, William J. Kennedy, and Clarence Allen, drew hundreds of town folks each night up until World War II while parking on opposite sides of Market Square. Hot dogs there were 7 cents a-piece.

Gilley has run the car, now owned by Mrs. Kennedy, since after the war. He first joined Kennedy, in the late 1920s. 'In those days, everyone wanted to hang around the streets nights. I had a job with the Post Office when I was a kid but decided to quit and take this job.'

Portsmouth's hot dog king hates to see the old gang die off. Some of the young ones never come back.

'I've seen the crews of three submarines, the S-4, the *Squalus*, and the *Thresher*, and other kinds who never came back,' the little Irishman sadly remembered.

He has seen others, too, who have thrown away promising future. Town inebriates know Gilley is a guy who will listen to their problems, but he won't let then cause trouble with other customers.

Gilley isn't in business to amass a fortune. He still makes his own hamburgers, cut his rolls, and chops onions to order.

Speaking of Kennedy, who died three year ago, he said, 'You know, the guy who used to own this place was a pretty good guy. He never worried about the cents. He figured if he had to be that close, then the hell with it—and he fed them from one coast to the other!'

Watching Gilley work on a busy day is an experience by itself. He works as fast as he talks, and business moves just a quickly. It's a wonder how time flies. You just get in the habit of it, that's all,' Gilley laughed with two missing front teeth showing.

Gilley is probably the only man in the world who gets a parking ticket every night. He pays it each night, too.

On cold winter evenings, Gilley's always a warm place to stop. The gas heater is steaming hot dogs which fog up the windows. Sleet and snow, a disaster, Gilley's is always there.

'Anything that's ever happened in town, we've always been in the middle of it. During all the fires, the gang's came around. Firemen run in for coffee and then back out again to fight the first. Yeah, we had some times.'

'Hey, Gilley, when are they going to put this wagon in Strawberry Banke' joked on customer.

'Yeah, they probably have it down there eventually,' he laughed.

Pushing 58, Gilley doesn't believe in retirement. 'How the hell can anyone retire? As long as you can still move around and feel good,' he states, 'there's no sense to it.'

'I got the horrors just hanging around last week,' he added referring to his illness. Characteristically wiping his brow and putting his hands on his hips Gilley concluded with a grin, 'That's life, chief!'

He turned and put on some more hot dogs. Portsmouth's legend of our time was back in business and it indispensable man was back to work.

Ralph 'Gilley' Gilbert had worked at the lunch cart for more than 40 years, dishing up hot dogs, sports scores, and local news to patrons. For several decades the cart got a nightly parking ticket in

Market Square. It moved to Fleet Street and Gilbert retired briefly following 'Gilley's Day,' a parade and celebration that drew nearly 2,000 people in 1974. Ralph 'Gilley' Gilbert died in 1986.

Red Arrow Hits Target, by Teri Dunn

(Courtesy of the Red Arrow Diner, Manchester, NH)

Sometimes you don't know what happened to you until after it's over. My recent breakfast visit to the Red Arrow Diner, a small, L-shaped, on-site diner in downtown Manchester, New Hampshire, was like that. That evening, back at home, I tucked into the piece of chocolate pie I'd asked for 'to go' not just because I am pie piggy, not because it was necessary for my 'research,' but because Carol Sheehan, the diner's owner, had proudly told me that her pastry chef Rachel McCullough makes all the pies 'daily, from scratch.' Last year between Thanksgiving and Christmas, other customers had taken home over 500 Red Arrow pies. Who was I to resist?

After all, eating chocolate pie on top of the splendid Eggs Benedict I'd had that morning would have been too much. I would've had to walk, or rather, stagger home! This turned out to be an outrageous concoction-silky chocolate cream ganache on the bottom layer, and a tower of chocolate-flavored real whipped cream, drizzled with chocolate syrup, atop that (it's called, if you must know, Death by Chocolate). Now I was far from the friendly, busy hubbub of this wonderful little diner. I was alone with the pie and a fork. But one bite brought it all back: Carol's friendly and vigorous diner management, the cleanliness and charm of the diner's interior, the efficient and cheerful staff...and the absolutely amazing food.

The Red Arrow is right downtown in Manchester, on a side street within walking distance of everything. Once upon a time, as with so many other cities along the meandering Merrimack River in New Hampshire and Massachusetts, this was a booming mill town. In those days, there were other Red Arrows, too, to serve the busy pace-one on Elm Street, one on West Merrimack Street, one on Lake Avenue, and one out on the Daniel Webster Highway. This one on Lowell Street is the sole survivor, having weathered Manchester's ups and downs. These days, the city is coming back; the mills have been converted to business and art lofts and housing, and tall buildings of banks and so forth have spouted-up downtown. The plucky little Lowell Street Red Arrow abides, having proudly fed the city's citizens through everything, and ready, willing and able to ride the wave of downtown Manchester's present revival. As an 'always open' focal point, it helps keep the neighborhood vital.

Carol and her staff make it impossible for you to forget the diner they all so obviously love and take pride in. There are lots of souvenirs, from t-shirts to mugs to lapel pins. Also, little wooden $1 off the next meal at the Red Arrow coins. And for the kids; yo-yos, paddleballs, Frisbees. You don't have to buy the kiddie stuff. Your child can win these things by coloring a drawing of the diner's signature happy-face Moe Mug, available at the diner or downloadable from the website. Or order a kiddie Blue Place Special meal; it comes on a plastic plate that turns out to be a Red Arrow Diner Frisbee your child can take home-how fun is that?!

As for the menu, it's very affordable and full of tradition and quality. All-day breakfast (famous baked beans with yout eggs? How about thick, succulent real Canadian bacon?), yes, bountiful burgers and sandwiches for lunch, yes, and yes, all your favorite dinner items from meatloaf to frank-and-beans to ale-battered fish to the night cook John Szwiec's teetering masterpiece lasagna

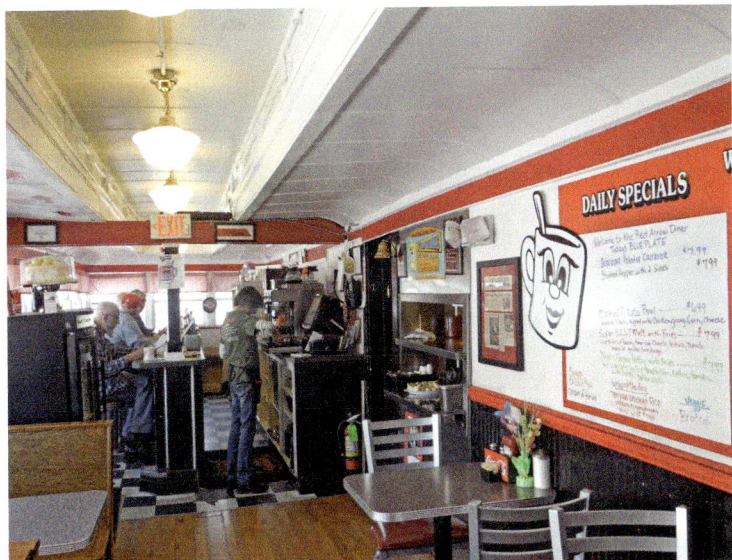

Whether or not you try the daily specials, you'll get a fantastic meal at the Red Arrow Diner in Milford, NH. *Photo courtesy of Carol Lawrence*

slabs. Many items are named after regulars, and Carol's kids and their friends. Daily specials 'sell like hotcake,' Carol says with a note of amazement in her voice. She should not be amazed, I think...she'd already told me she stocks the kitchen with excellent ingredients, and when they get into the capable hands of Rachel or John or her prep cook Anival Pascaval, Consistency and marvelous quality combine to make wonderful meals.

When carol showed me around the diner, including the tiny but streamlined kitchen and the bakery/office area in the basement, she took the time to greet each and every one of her staffers and make a point of introducing them to me. Back out front, my server was one of those rare waitresses that expertly gauges when you are ready to order, when you need more water, and when you need a question answered-all on instinct.

Getting everyone invested in the diner, from staff to customers, is clearly Carol's recipe for success. She's owned the Red Arrow for many years and she takes care to acknowledge and respect those who've contributed to the diner's history. She's posted a series of vintage photographs on the walls and recounts tales of the beloved past owner Levi Letendre in her informal diner newsletter (which appeals to customers for 'more tales and any photos' to be rewarded with diner gift certificates). The 'Moe' logo was supplied many years ago by a regular customer named Moe; then came a call to supply a gal pal. But instead of naming her herself, Carol involved the customers again and held a contest. The winning party? 'Dinah.'

The Red Arrows future is assured by only tweaking a winning formula. For instance, the diner went smoke free in 1998, even though New Hampshire law did not require it. It 'felt risky at first,' Carol remembers, but she's been vindicated by a 20-percent boost in business. More recently, she's instituted a lively, interesting, interactive website, which nurtures the diner's sense of community with plentiful contributions from staff and customers.

As for the present, the place hums like a well-oiled machine, day in and day out, 7 days a week (closed briefly in the afternoon on Christmas eve and reopening the following morning) The Red Arrow is a happy and busy place because everybody is welcome, old, young, townie, and tourist.

I can't wait to go back. I wish I could meet the night cook John (who, when not working or getting much deserved rest, is an avid bicycler and contributes a rambling philosophical blog-diary to the website) (if you stop him as he peddles by, he will give you a few of those '$1 off your next Red Arrow meal'). I wish I could try another slice of Rachel's pie...I hear the Coconut Cream is outstanding. But most of all I wish the Red Arrow to be there forever, nourishing everyone who comes through its narrow door and into that welcoming little space, body and soul. This fun, beautiful run diner is truly what is best about American diners, a treasure to be treasured.

Thank you Carol.

Friday Night at the Local Diner, by Bruce Heald

It's Friday night and the high school basketball game is over. Many of us hurriedly race down to the Main Street Diner for an evening burger, soda and maybe a hot cup of coffee for the folks.

A typical classic Worcester Diner of the Forties, and we all prop ourselves on a stool at the counter, and relax at the booths near the side windows. It seems like everyone in town shows up for a late snack. At the booth, double dating high school couples practice politeness and manners.

We are all greeted by Carl, the side-order cook, aproned and ready for some action. He spins on his heels, takes our order and sings out the order to the kitchen or performs at the grill for two hamburgers, side order of fries, four hot dogs and a large serving of fried dough. The waitress races over to the booth and takes the order. Every once and a while a slip will float into the back kitchen with an unapologetic order for a cheeseburger and fries or a full plate order of meat loaf and mashed potatoes drenched in gravy. All the orders are received and treated with the utmost respect. After all, the homely dishes are the mainstay of the better diners in all of New Hampshire.

The typical proprietors of the village diners have not turned their back on its traditional classic diners. Most of the present owner of the diners didn't want to turn their place into upscale, gourmet, reservation type of eating places.

Here at the Main Street Diner, the meals that are prepared are usually diner fare. The cook arranges a plate of chicken salad on a bed of greens, then fixes another of pork tenderloin with a side of mango chutney, bright and mouthwatering against the sparkling white plate. Next is served a hefty portion of piping-hot fiddlehead lasagna, then scoops an order of Tuscan black-backed sole out of the oven and served it with brilliant Oriental greens tossed in a light vinaigrette. These are specials for the Vietnamese clientele.

On most and given Friday nights, many of our guests seem to fit the thirty something profile, young professionals in search of a real food at down-to-earth prices. But there are those older couples sipping coffee or nursing a large wedge of apple pie. Nobody really knows, but Friday nights are always interesting. There's good energy on these nights.

I notice in the far corner booth two women have met for dinner as they do every Friday night. They always order the same dish (the Blue Plate special) and the other a roast-beef diner with all the trimmin's.

This diner has been serving the same food for forty years, and some of our customers have been coming in for nearly that long.

Our diner is the center of town gatherings, political campaigning or a mid-night snack when all is closed, but the diners are open.

The Customers' Notes

For almost twenty years my deceased husband owned a small Worcester Diner in the North Country. It was known as the Main Street Diner, for obvious reasons, but today the name has changed. He told stories of what he served: Mothers old-fashioned Baked Beans. Blue Lake String Beans, etc. His customers were told that the Maple Syrup for the pancakes came from a tree he owned from across the river in Vermont. Every holiday the cook, waitresses, and he would decorate and dress for the occasion. He spoke of his customers that came in who were nice, from different companies, on their lunch hour as his guests, and the customers from across the tracks, they were gangsters.

He told many stories that his children could probably tell better then I, because they even worked there for a time during their school years. It gave him a good and happy life for those years and helped him put his children through college. Darn-it—I miss him and the old diner.

Posted by anonymous on July 1, 2010

I beg to differ. The original "lunch cart" occupied by the Nite Owl Diner in Fall River, Massachusetts was definitely NOT demolished. My parents took me to both locations throughout my childhood for the best Hot Cheese Sandwich I've ever eaten. As a frequent diner at the Nite Owl, I am now craving a good old fashioned Hot Cheese Sandwich . . . ooo the beautiful gooey melted cheese with mustard and a thin slice of onion. I've tried to duplicate that flavor many times over the years with no success. I don't care about cholesterol. I need a Hot Cheese fix, please???

Posted by Joyce Terry on July 1, 2010

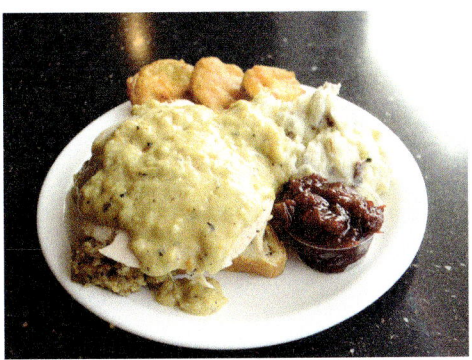
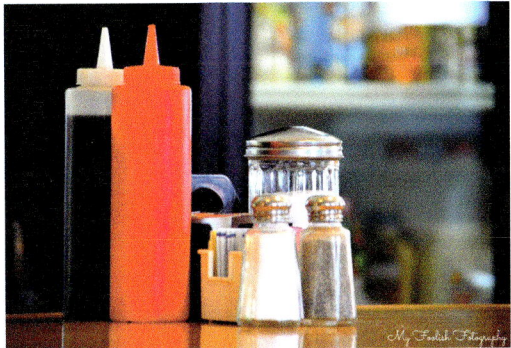

Left: Roundabout-turkey. *Photo courtesy of the Roundabout Diner*
Right: Colorful condiments at the Olde Bay Diner. *Photo courtesy of the Olde Bay Diner*

Trivia

Boy Scouts

Darcy and Jim's Diner was located in the White Mountains about 20 miles from their home. It was a real railroad car with an extra room added on the back.

We served delicious homemade pies and sold large slices for twenty cents.

I had no experience in the food business, but I learned very quickly. It was interesting waiting on tourists and the local folks. The most challenging day came when two buses of young boy scouts stopped. Each boy ordered a hamburger and a milkshake—to be made on the one shake machine I owned with hard ice cream! We all sighed when they drove away, and then grabbed our brooms.

A Table for Two

It was my senior year in high school—class of 1954. I worked in the Main Street Diner during weeknights and weekends.

I spent a lot of time with my husband-to-be at the time. He lived about 10 miles out in the country and often drove into town in his dad's logging truck. He would come to the diner, pick a stool, and order his favorite: a hamburger and a chocolate milkshake. Only I could make his milkshake just as he liked it. (I would give it a few extra squirts of chocolate when my boss wasn't looking.)

He would stay and watch me work, waiting until I got off so he could walk me home. But before we left, we would sit at our favorite table in the window, gazing into each other's eyes as we listened to "Hello Darlin" by Conway Twitty on the jukebox.

Specialty Steakburgers

I grew up in a little town near the Canadian border. During my high school years, I worked in a little trailer-house diner called Ma Smith's Steakburgers She did not call them hamburgers; she had the meat ground up specially and dubbed the "steakburgers".

The menu consisted of steakburgers, potato salad, baked beans, chips, ice cream, coffee, tea and soft drinks. Ma Smith made the best potato salad I have ever eaten, and she taught me how to make it. I still prepare potato salad the same way, and my family and friends love it.

In the summertime, Ma Smith would put a radio in an open window, and the kids would all come to dance to the music on the sand and gravel in the front driveway of the diner. What a swell time we all had!

Diner Lingo

The language of the diner is entertaining and very descriptive. If you listen carefully you may understand the lingo that is commonly used in the diner. Try it—you might enjoy it! (*Compliments of the C-Man Restaurants*)

Compliments of the C-Man Restaurants.
Cow feed = Salad
Bubble dancer = Dishwasher
Hockey puck = Well-done hamburger
Cluck and grunt = Eggs & bacon
Barley water = Beer
Motor oil = Syrup
First lady = An order of ribs
Bow-wow = Hot dog
Yum-yum = Sugar
Two dots and a dash = Two fried eggs & a strip of bacon
Walk a cow through the garden = Burger with lettuce, tomato & onion
Black cow = Chocolate milk & milkshake
Butcher's revenge = Meatloaf
Mike and Ike = Salt & peppers shakers
Eve with a lid on = Apple pie
Make it moo = Add milk to coffee
Cowboy with spurs = Western omelet with French Fries
Swamp water = Soda made with all flavors available
Whistle berries = Baked beans
Dirty water = Coffee
Yellow paint = Mustard
Battery acid = Grapefruit juice
Adam and Eve on a raft = Two poached eggs on toast
Moo juice = Milk
Fish eyes = Tapioca pudding
Cow paste = Butter
Soup jockey = Waitress
City juice = Water
Birdseed = Breakfast cereal
Nervous pudding = Bowl of Jell-O
Bronx vanilla = Garlic
Hold the grass = No lettuce

Classic Diner Food—When & Where

The excellence of the classic diner Food in New Hampshire is not the least of its attractions of our visitors. For many of them, the food is one of the chief delights of a holiday or weekend vacation.

I've spent a good deal of time traveling and studying the Granite State's appeal and trying to be as helpful as possible to all readers who like to visit our lakes and mountains, historic landmarks and good places to have a fine American meal. I certainly wouldn't travel throughout the state as happily as I like to, if the food was not interesting and the country atmosphere so appealing.

There are various conceptions, in New Hampshire, of what constitutes good food, of what a man may eat for his stomach's sake, and even for his soul's sake.

New Hampshire food in the early days of the local town diners was a time when pies were a breakfast item. One of my local friends informed me that you're not a native unless you eat apple pie and ice cream for breakfast. But I am sure you need not expect to meet any early-morning pies. And if you are one of those who think baked beans are "as nasty as they look," or who quake at the mere mention of a New England boiled dinner, you may travel the length and breadth of New Hampshire without an encounter to distress you. If New Hampshire food has a fault nowadays it has its roots I think, in the desire of many restaurant proprietors to cater to all tastes. Superior cooking, in my opinion, consists less in thinking up and concocting something that no one ever concocted before, than in preparing an established favorite in some superlatively satisfying way.

I frequently wish that schools of domestic science and New Hampshire's diners would concentrate more on hash, hamburgers and good breakfasts.

I can't promise you that you'll meet no fantastic concoctions in New England prepared for you in misguided zeal to tempt your unpredictable appetite, but I believe I can promise that you'll never find yourself in a pinch where you have to eat them.

New Hampshire abounds in delicious eateries, the classic diners, where the food is fresh, home grown and cooked well for the royal family. I don't know of any diner in New Hampshire I don't like. Most diners are basic American food.

Down in Portsmouth, there is a fine up-class diner called the Roundabout, which serves notable sea food: lobster roll, clams, oysters, scallops, and for the land-lovers, the Phantom Gourmet barbecue.

Not far away from the Roundabout in Portsmouth is Gilley's Diner which serves the finest hamburger you'll ever eat at reasonable prices.

Everyone knows the sweet taste of maple syrup and maple sugar, but not everyone has learned the many varieties, the toothsomeness, of soft maple sugar or maple cream as a spread for waffles and pancakes, and on oatmeal in the morning. Then you must go north to the Littleton Diner in Littleton, New Hampshire—they have the best in the state. Or head to Route 104 in New Hampton for home-cooked meatloaf and shepherd's pie. For lunch, take a fifteen minute ride over to Rumney on Rte. 25, where American home cooking is from the pan, not the can. At the Four Acres in Lebanon, you will find the finest home fries with melted cheese as well as homemade cakes, pies and huge doughnuts. On your way south on I-93, exit 20, stop and enjoy some shepherd's pie with good classic diner atmosphere.

There are many diners in New Hampshire I'd like to sing the praises of, from their food to their atmosphere, to their outstanding service. But the best I can do is to say in plain English—although I have eaten superlative food in many lands, I feel lyric about the food of the *Classic Diners of New Hampshire*.

List of Diners in New Hampshire

Airport Diner (C-Man)
2280 Brown Avenue
Manchester, NH 03101

Andre's Diner
100 Willow St.
Manchester, NH 03103

Betty's Kitchen
164 Lafayette Rd.
Hampton, NH 03842

Center Harbor Diner
17 Whittier Hwy, Tr. 25
Moultonborough, NH 03254

Cote's Diner
1 Pinard St.
Manchester, NH 03101

Bristol Diner
33 So. Main Street
Bristol, NH 03222

Daddypops Tumble Inn Diner
1 Main Street
Claremont, NH 03743

Derry Diner
29 Crystal Avenue,
Derry, NH 03038

Donna Jean's Diner
1208 Weirs Blvd.
Laconia, NH 03246

Fast Eddie's Diner
320 Lafayette Rd.
Hampton, NH 03842

Four Acres Diner
23 Bridge St. (Rte. 4)
West Lebanon, NH 03784

George's Diner
10 Plymouth St.
Meredith, NH 03253

Gilley's PM Lunch
175 Fleet St.
Portsmouth, NH 03801

Heritage Diner
Main St.
Charlestown, NH 03603

Hillsborough Diner
83 Henniker St.
Hillsborough, NH

Hope Diner
127 Plaistow Rd.
Plaistow, NH 03865

Joey's Diner
1 Craftsman Lane
Amherst, NH 03031

Lindy's Diner
9 Gilbo St.
Keene, NH 03431

Littleton Diner
170 Maine St.
Littleton, NH 03561

Main Street Station Diner
Main Street
Plymouth, NH 03264

Margie's Dream Diner
172 Harward St.
Manchester, NH 0300103

Market Place Diner
4 Village Market Place
Hollis, NH 03049

Mary Ann's Diner
29 E. Broadway
Derry, NH 03038

Meredith Diner
Main St.
Meredith, NH 03253

Miss Wakefield Diner
7 Windy Hollow Rd.
Sanbornville, NH 03872

Mt. Pisgah Diner
118 Main Street
Winchester, NH 03470

Old Bay Diner
Rt. 11
Alton Bay, NH 03809

Peterboro Diner
10 Depot Rd.
Peterborough, NH 03458

Pink Cadillac
17d Farmington Rd.
Rochester, NH 03867

Plain Jane's Diner
897 Rte. 25
Rumney, NH 03266

Red Arrow Diner
61 Lowell St.
Manchester, NH 03101

Red Arrow Diner
63 Union Square
Milford, NH 03055

Roundabout Diner
580 US 1
(Portsmouth Traffic Circle)
Portsmouth, NH 03801

Route 104 Diner
752 Rte. 104
New Hampton, NH 03862

Shore Diner
Rte. 3 Laconia, NH 03246

Sunny Day Diner
Rte. 3 (Connector Rd.)
Lincoln, NH 03251

Swanzey Diner
515 Monadnock Hwy 11
Keene, NH 03431

Tilt'n Diner (C-Man)
61 Laconia Rd.
Tilton, NH 03276

Union Diner (Paugus Diner)
1331 Union Avenue
Laconia, NH 03246

Wolfeborough Diner
5 North Main Street
Wolfeboro, NH 03894

Railroad Diners
Café Lafayette (Hobo Railroad Dinner Car)
Lincoln, NH 93251

Conway Scenic Railroad
Main St. No. Conway, NH

Winnipesaukee Railroad (Hobo)
So. Main Street
Meredith, NH 03253

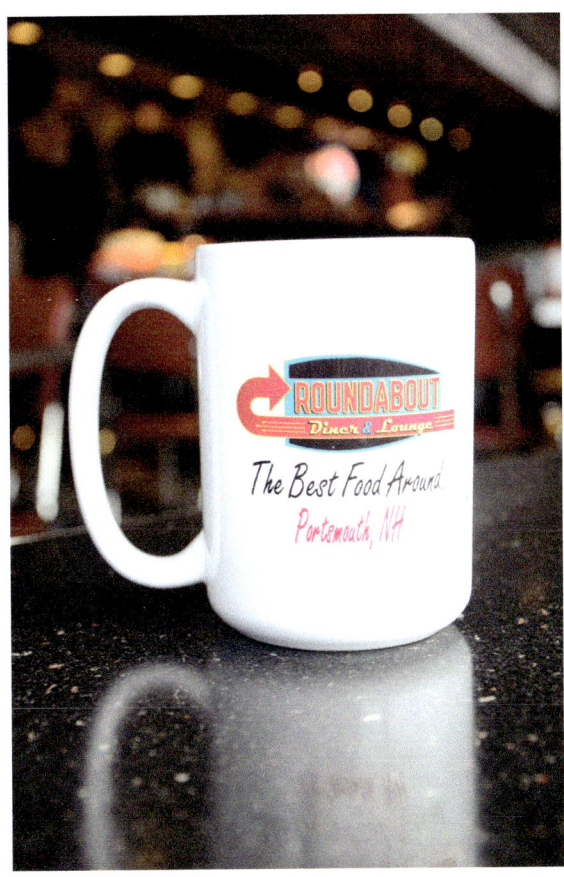

Dinerised porcelain mug at the Roundabout Diner. *Courtesy the Roundabout Diner*

Bibliography

Brady, A. J.; Nutrition. A Public Demand Diner, *American Restaurant Magazine*; 1947.

Ewen, Stuart, *Captains of Consciousness*, New York, 1976.

Flynn, Mike; *I Just Got Back From Lunch*, address unknown, Diner Archives, 1946.

Fodero, Pat; Market Analysis of the Restaurant Industry, New York, *American Restaurant Magazine*, September 17, 1993.

Fuller, Bruce; Gilley's Back on the Square, Portsmouth, New Hampshire, *Portsmouth Herald*, date unknown.

Garbin, Randy; *Diners of New England*, Mechanicsburg, PA: Stackpole Books, 2005.

Gutman, Richard J. S.; *American Diner: Then and Now*. New York: Harper Perennial, 1993.

Hurley, Andrew; Interview with George Yonko, May 1994,—From Hash House to Family Restaurant. New York, *Journal of American History*, 1997.

Hersman, Earle; interview with Hurley: Chip Silverman, Diner Guys, New York; 1989

Jackson, Donald D., The American is in Decline, yet more Chic than Ever, Washington, DC, Smithsonian, No. 86., Vol. 17 Issue, 1986.

Kaplin, Donald and Bellink; Boston, MA. *Classic Diners of the Northeast*, London, England, Faber & Faber, 1986.

Kullman, Harold; interview by Hurley; 1993.

Langdon, *Orange Roofs, Golden Arches*, San Francisco, CA; 1985.

Levenstein, Harvey; *Paradox of Plenty: A Social History of Eating in Modern America*, New York, *American Restaurant Magazine*; 1993.

Matyas, Jo.; Kingston Diners, Ontario, Canada, *The Star*, 2007.

Offitzer, Karen, Diners, New York: New Line Books; 2002.

Susman, Warren, Interview with Edward Griffin. Chicago, IL; 1989.

Tierney, Patrick J., *The Tierney Book of opportunity*, New Rochelle, NY. P. J. Tierney Sons. Inc. 1924

United States Bureau of Census, Cause of Population, Vol. III. 1950.